THE
7 LOVE
AGREEMENTS

DOUGLAS WEISS, PhD

SILOAM
A STRANG COMPANY

Most STRANG COMMUNICATIONS/CHARISMA HOUSE/SILOAM products are available at special quantity discounts for bulk purchase for sales promotions, premiums, fund-raising, and educational needs. For details, write Strang Communications/Charisma House/Siloam, 600 Rinehart Road, Lake Mary, Florida 32746, or telephone (407) 333-0600.

THE 7 LOVE AGREEMENTS by Douglas Weiss, PhD
Published by Siloam
A Strang Company
600 Rinehart Road
Lake Mary, Florida 32746
www.siloam.com

Unless otherwise noted, all Scripture quotations are from the Holy Bible, New International Version. Copyright © 1973, 1978, 1984, International Bible Society. Used by permission.

Scripture quotations marked KJV are from the King James Version of the Bible.

Scripture quotations marked NKJV are from the New King James Version of the Bible. Copyright © 1979, 1980, 1982 by Thomas Nelson, Inc., publishers. Used by permission.

Cover design by Judith McKittrick; cover image © 2005 JupiterImages Corporation; interior design by Terry Clifton

Library of Congress Cataloging-in-Publication Data:
Weiss, Douglas.
  The 7 love agreements / Doug Weiss.
    p. cm.
  ISBN 1-59185-724-4 (hardback)
  1. Love--Religious aspects--Christianity. 2. Marriage--Religious aspects--Christianity. I. Title.
BV4639.W39 2005
248.8'44--dc22

                                        2005016575

                                      First Edition

                        05 06 07 08 09 — 987654321
                      Printed in the United States of America

People and incidents in this book are composites created by the author from his experiences in counseling. Names and details of the stories have been changed, and any similarity between the names and stories of individuals described in this book to individuals known to readers is purely coincidental.

TO THE HEROES
WHO HOLD THE HAND OF
THEIR BELOVED ALL
THE DAYS OF THEIR LIVES

CONTENTS

A better, more intimate

marriage relationship is a

matter of the heart.

Chapter One

THE LOVE AGREEMENTS

I had just finished speaking at a marriage conference when a cou-ple walked toward me. As I took a deep breath, I wondered: *Are they coming to me with a thirty-year-old marital problem, or do they have an issue regarding a son or daughter?* As we began to talk, I discovered that Lorraine and Scott were small group leaders in a good-sized church in the Midwest.

Scott looked overwhelmed as he started to share. "Dr. Doug," he told me, "I have a guy in our small group, and he and his wife are having major problems. You see, they haven't been physically intimate in years. They don't do anything together. As a matter of fact, they don't even eat meals together."

I probably looked slightly surprised. Although I have coun-seled many couples who have similar difficulties, this was taking "not liking each other" to a whole new level. Scott told me that this couple attended church regularly, and both of them claimed Jesus as

Lord. The man attended Scott's cell group weekly, and his wife also attended a small group meeting regularly.

This couple started marriage just like so many other couples who struggle in the same area. They were in their early twenties when they met at a church singles group. At the beginning of their relationship, they socialized with other singles from their church, often enjoying the company of others, and each other, until late in the evening.

Eventually they paired off from the singles group and started to date. They invested in long walks, eating together, and having long talks in the car like most of us. They prayed and sought the Lord and believed they were to marry. They sought the advice of their pastors, friends, and family, and everyone seemed to think this was a great idea.

She walked down the aisle to the familiar tune of "The Wedding March," as millions of other brides have done. She was beautiful; he was handsome; and they literally drove off into the sunset.

Life appeared normal. They went to work, paid their bills, and went to church. After the first child, things changed significantly. Each other's faults became the source of conversations. The blame game began. Stress, fatigue, and family responsibilities grew. Each individual began to retreat into his or her own world. He focused on work. She focused on the children. Neither focused on each other or the marriage.

Over time, their distance toward each other turned into silence.

Yes, they were married on paper, but slowly their hearts grew cold toward each other.

Fast forward to today, and this couple was now experiencing an empty, heartless marriage relationship—and they both felt stuck as to what to do about it.

"Wow!" you may say. Right now you may be thanking God that you are not experiencing the same difficulties in your marriage relationship. Like you, I am also glad that doesn't describe my marriage. I personally enjoy eating meals and playing together with Lisa, my wife of nineteen years. I love looking into her eyes and seeing the joy in her smile. The fragrance of Lisa is everywhere in my life.

You probably enjoy a good meal with your spouse as well. You may have your favorite restaurant that you enjoy together, and even your favorite stories to tell. But how do you make sure that you stay happy together for the rest of your lives? There is one important principle to understand first. It is this: *A better, more intimate marriage relationship is a matter of the heart.*

YOUR HEART MATTERS

Yes, within the heart is where a marriage either is made healthy or slowly deteriorates. To help us understand this, we will take a closer look at the heart.

Proverbs 23:7 states: "For as [a man] thinketh in his heart, so is he" (KJV). We are also told to "keep your heart with all diligence, for out of it spring the issues of life" (Prov. 4:23, NKJV).

This vital organ, your heart, is so important to your marriage. In

Scripture the heart is often referred to as the location of your mind, your will, and your emotions. It is vital to understand each of these three elements in relationship to the heart.

Your mind

Your mind is one of God's greatest achievements of creation. Your mind is like a vast computer, much faster and with greater storage capacity than anything created by man to date. In this small organ is stored the details of every experience you have ever had. Your mind stores a photograph of every place you have ever visited in your lifetime, as well as a picture of every person you have ever met. Also, in your mind is recorded every word you have ever spoken and every word you have ever heard.

This tremendous storage capacity is not the only great thing about your mind. Your mind can review all the stored data, search through all the experiences, ideas, and conversations you have ever had, and merge it all together *in a fraction of a second*, allowing you to communicate and make decisions instantly. Yet, it is amazing that this massive mind of yours comprises only one-third of the function of your heart.

Your will

The human will is absolutely astonishing. Because of the human will, individuals have climbed the highest mountains, ran long distances, created unimaginable technology, and designed vast highways and cities beyond imagination. Your will provides the raw fuel your heart needs to carry out the instructions you, as the owner of your heart, command.

Your will is incredibly capable of both great good or great unkindness.

Your emotions

The third component of your heart is your emotions, another vast territory. Emotions are the way that you experience life and make a connection with your environment, with others, and even with yourself. Emotions, also known as *feelings*, can be very tricky. Most of us have had no training on how to have, identify, or communicate our feelings. For so many people, feelings are a real mystery. If this is also difficult for you, I strongly recommend that you read my book *Intimacy: A 100-Day Guide to Better Relationships* for a more in-depth look into the area of feelings.[1]

We all need to be able to have, identify, and communicate the hundreds of feelings we experience. Feelings can be conflicting in that you can feel two opposing feelings at the same time. Feelings can also happen at an incredible, almost overwhelming rate. Feelings are transitory. No feeling lasts forever. They all leave at some point.

Feelings are not facts. You can *feel* fat and yet not have gained a pound. You can have a PhD, yet still not feel very bright. (This happens to me every time I walk into Home Depot.) Feelings are amazing. They flood the human heart and make so many of the experiences you have wonderful, satisfying events in your life.

God Himself has feelings. You can't read the Scriptures without feeling His fury, compassion, patience, and love. Like Himself, God has created us to have feelings and a heart that possess a great mind, will, and emotions.

AGREEMENTS

The heart is not only the location of your mind, will, and emotions. It is also the place where you make agreements. These agreements are a powerful aspect of your heart.

Once your heart makes an agreement, it sends out an edict to the mind, the will, and the emotions. The agreement commands great power over your heart. Once an agreement has been made, only another agreement can break it.

Let me give you a couple of examples of the power of an agreement. As a counselor, I have heard hundreds of stories about people who have made agreements throughout their life. Carlos grew up in Juarez, Mexico. His family was very poor. He remembers many days when he went without food. Many times he was unable even to take a bath. One day, some boys who came from wealthier families made fun of Carlos's clothes. They taunted him, making fun of the fact that he was just a poor boy. Only eight years old, Carlos ran away from them into an alley where he crouched down on the hot sweltering pavement. As he cried, he made an agreement in his heart, *When I grow up, I will never be poor.*

Carlos made sure he learned English. He studied hard to get a scholarship to college. He worked in the summer and saved as much money as he could. He went to college and, upon graduation, applied for a visa the first day after he graduated so he could legally come to the United States. He worked hard in America and began his own company. He became an American citizen and was successful in a couple of businesses.

He married and had three beautiful children. But he was never home, continually working day and night. By the time he was in his late forties, he was worth over fifteen million dollars. He kept his agreement, but he couldn't stop working. He barely knew his children, and his wife was ready to leave. Carlos did not understand the effect that earlier agreement was having in controlling his current life.

Agreements of the heart have great power. By looking back at the story at the beginning of this chapter that Lorraine and Scott told me at the conference, we discover that somewhere along the way, that husband and wife had made some powerful agreements. They made agreements not to forgive, not to be patient, not to serve, respect, or not to be kind to each other.

Deep in their hearts each of these individuals had made some destructive agreements that were tearing their marriage relationship apart. In Amos 3:3 we read these words: "Can two walk together, unless they are agreed?" (NKJV).

This couple had subjected the vast power of their minds, wills, and emotions under the direction of agreements not to love each other. Day in and day out they were withholding hugs, kisses, sex, compliments, acts of kindness, and service from one another. The effect of these decisions is absolutely mind-boggling. How do you wake up day after day and not touch or talk to each other? Can you imagine the great commitment they have dedicated to these destructive agreements?

This couple used the tremendous storage capacity of their minds to store up endless scores of wrongdoing. They used their wills to avoid each other—even though they lived in the same house. They used their emotions to feel contempt for each other.

This couple had truly learned the power of agreement. However, here is the problem: they were using the secret power of their heart to make *destructive* agreements, those that had the power to *destroy a marriage* as opposed to *building a great marriage*.

WE HAVE THE POWER

God has given each one of us the power to make and carry out our agreements. We choose whether we are going to invest this power in a positive agreement or a destructive one. The events of September 11, 2001 began when one heart determined to make an agreement to hate and kill others. Yet, it was also the power that Mother Theresa invested in a positive agreement that enabled her to love the millions of unlovable people whose lives she touched for good in India. Both individuals had been created by God with one heart. Both made agreements in their hearts, and both successfully carried out those agreements.

You too have a heart—a great big heart capable of incredible constructive or destructive achievements.

You may have a spouse who is also reading these pages. The agreements that the two of you make regarding your relationship, which we will be calling *love agreements* throughout this book, are critical.

The love agreements you make or don't make in your life can be the difference between having a great loving marriage or a distant, cold marriage.

Your love agreements will show up in your day-to-day behaviors, just as Carlos's agreement not to be poor influenced his daily life. Like him, day in and day out, you will live out the agreements you make.

In this book I am introducing you to seven love agreements that will dispose you to greater intimacy with God and with your spouse. Making the love agreements does not guarantee instant results. But they launch us on a process of bettering our marriage relationship. The process works best when wife and husband choose the behaviors together. But one partner can make the agreements solo as a way of drawing closer to his or her spouse.

The love agreements are not once-for-all promises. We do not pledge to always be faithful, patient, or kind, because we will sometimes fail. Better to review and renew the agreements frequently, perhaps even daily. One day at a time builds love and intimacy. "Always" slides into failure and discouragement.

Here are the seven love agreements we will take a close look at in the following chapters:

THE SEVEN LOVE AGREEMENTS

1. *Faithfulness.* I will be faithful to my spouse at all times and in all circumstances.

2. *Patience.* I will not try to change things about my spouse that I do not like but will modify my behaviors that annoy my partner.

3. *Forgiveness.* When I have offended my spouse, I will quickly ask for forgiveness. And I will forgive my spouse's offenses in my heart even before being asked.

4. *Service.* I will anticipate my spouse's spiritual, emotional, physical, and material needs and will do everything I can to meet them.

5. *Respect.* I will not act or speak in a way that demeans, ridicules, or embarrasses my spouse.

6. *Kindness.* I will be kind to my spouse, eliminating any trace of meanness from my behavior and speech.

7. *Celebration.* I will appreciate my spouse's gifts and attributes and celebrate them personally and publicly.

When you fully understand these seven love agreements, you can direct or correct the course of your marriage. When you understand the love agreements, you can realize that *you can make heartfelt choices that orient your will to act more Christianly toward your spouse.*

REALITY

Love agreements are real. You make them, and you carry them out. Once you have made these love agreements in your heart, the day-to-day behavior will begin to follow. As you make the love agreements, you will see different behaviors and attitudes show up in your marriage. *Aiming at higher standards of behavior opens us up to improvement.*

Everyone has heard the saying, "If you aim at nothing, you'll hit it." I've heard several motivational speakers and pastors express the need for focus or aiming for goals. As Christians *we ought to aim for the stars in our marriage—even if you feel as if you are only hitting the tops of the trees.* At least you are headed in the right direction. And remember this: the tops of the trees are higher than the ground from which you started.

Let's suppose that we know a guy named Luke who is making the love agreement to be patient. So he is going through his day focused on his agreement. When his wife is late once again from work, he chooses not to say anything. While she's talking on the phone to her sister when it's bedtime for the children, he writes a kind note, "Your children want your special hugs." He avoids making the unkind remark that he would normally give her, saying, "Get off the phone and help me, NOW!"

You can see that Luke's love agreement is starting to show up in his behavior. He is not giving his wife the typical look that says, *Get off the phone!* Luke is focused.

Even though Luke is the one making the love agreement, it impacts their whole night together. Luke has avoided his usual questioning about why she is late and the shaming of his bride for being her typical fifteen to thirty minutes late. As a result, his wife avoided her traditional comment: "You're a selfish husband! Can't you deal with the children for even a few minutes?" This is turning out to be a different day, and Luke feels good because he knows he has contributed to making it a better day for both of them.

Once you make a love agreement, you place your heart on a different path. You begin to look for opportunities to practice the behavior prompted by the particular love agreement you have made. You start to find ways to improve in *yourself.* Improvement in you introduces a completely different dynamic into your marriage relationship.

I attended many twelve-step type meetings as a mental health technician in a chemical dependency unit in Texas years ago. I would drive my clients to their groups and sit inside to monitor the clients and be able to process with them the content of the group.

There were several times when an old-timer in Alcoholics Anonymous (AA) would chime in and say something like, "You know, I've learned I had to try something different. It didn't really matter what different was; I just knew I couldn't keep doing the same old thing and get different results." We would all laugh, and the group would acknowledge the wisdom of the old timer's words.

This wisdom is true in marriage as well. *Trying something different gets different results.* Often counselors offer different strategies for a spouse than the ones previously tried. When that person tries the new technique or phrase, he or she gets different results.

THE DIFFERENCE

Part of the promise underlying the love agreements is their offer of something different. If you will try making one of the love agreements, you will be able to test and see if your agreement can change the way you and your spouse interact. Like Luke, you may discover the experience of a completely different evening spent with your spouse because you made that love agreement.

Most books that are written about marriage tend to focus on things a couple can do together to make their marriage better. This is where the love agreements I'm talking about in this book are different—*you can do them without your spouse!*

Committing to these love agreements as a couple is great if both you and your spouse are equally motivated at the same time to improve your marriage. But even if your spouse does not appear to want to make a love agreement, you can commit to one or all of these agreements yourself—and you can expect to see results that will impact both of you in your relationship to one another.

Let me share something I learned in a Wise Counsel Meeting I attended. Wise Counsel is a group of businessmen with whom I am privileged to meet quarterly. We discuss our business plans and also discuss heart issues with each other. We believe in the idea of iron sharpening iron. One day one of these great men was sharing a big business idea. As part of the Wise Counsel process, we began to ask questions and give feedback.

One of the men made a profound statement that has meant a lot to me over the years. He said, "It sounds like your plan depends on too many people to be successful." He continued by stating that he had learned that the more people it took to make something successful, the less likely it was to be successful.

Another guy explained it this way: "Getting two planets to line up is easier than getting eight planets to line up." I hope you're catching this idea. Many marriage books make the assumption that both people in the marriage are motivated to change. They assume both people are going to have the same level of commitment and perseverance to make the suggested changes and do whatever exercises the author suggests.

The love agreements come from a totally different perspective. I don't begin with an assumption that both you and your spouse are equally motivated to change. I also don't want to assume that both of you will have the same level of perseverance to reach the same goals.

Being a counselor for more than seventeen years, I have learned a lot. Practical day-in-day-out experiences counseling clients has cautioned me to make this assumption. Some couples who come to my office have obviously scheduled the visit because only one person is motivated to change. Only one person is experiencing pain due to the lack of connectedness or intimacy. One person is at a near-breaking point, while the other spouse is oblivious to the marital problem.

In marriage, couples are often motivated at different times to change. I've heard more than once from couples that they talked about getting marriage counseling for years. When I ask about this, they tell me they could never both agree to seek counseling at the same time.

Often one person in the marriage does not have the same level of commitment as the other. Let's consider that Tony and Julie are a typical couple who have come to my office. In our counseling session, Tony and Julie discuss the issues they want resolved. They are given homework assignments to do. I am aware as they leave my office that one of them will not follow through with the assignment. During the weeks of counsel, repeatedly one completes the assignment and the other does not.

So even though they both came for marriage counseling, both did not have the same level of perseverance to change. That's where the love agreements differ from the principles for changes in a traditional marriage book. I am not depending on cooperation from both you and your spouse to get to a better marriage—although that would probably make for faster change.

A love agreement depends solely on one heart to make it work. One heart harnesses the vast resources of the mind, will, and emotions. The love agreements are not focused on changing both of you. The love agreements are a system of doing marriage right. The love agreements focus on you, your heart, and you doing your marriage right.

Like Luke, as you individually commit to these love agreements, your commitment will be the catalyst to many different days, evenings, and weekends with your spouse that make a difference in your marriage relationship. In Luke's case, his wife didn't do anything to make things different. She was late as usual and was on the phone as Luke helped the children brush their teeth, wash their faces, and put on their pajamas. Yet there was a marked change in their relationship.

You can make a big difference in your marriage. I know from personal experience that when I change my behavior, it changes our day. If I can practice my love agreements, then Lisa and I can have a better day.

What I like about the love agreements is that I don't need my spouse to agree to anything. Lisa can continue along her merry way, and she might not notice the love agreement I made right away. But eventually she and others catch on. "You're acting differently," she may comment.

If your spouse says something like this, you just smile and say, "Is that a good thing?"

"Yes, yes," your spouse reassures you. And, although it may take a longer time than it took for your spouse to notice the difference in you, soon you may begin noticing that he or she has also chosen to make a love agreement of his or her own.

In Luke's case, it may take months for his wife to notice that he doesn't complain when she is late. In time, she might appreciate this change. Further down the road she might want to be on time or early just because she likes her patient husband. All of this happens because Luke made one love agreement and changed the whole system.

Marriage is many things, but one thing it is for sure is a system of verbal and nonverbal communication. It's a system of pushing buttons and getting known results. You act one way, which influences the other person to act another way. All of us who are married have created systems. You know that if a man buys flowers just to show his love, there is a system. He gives the flowers, and she gives a kiss.

Couples can have hundreds of systems at work in their relationship. Some couples have a system whereby one spouse leaves the dirty clothes and towels on the floor, and the other spouse complains but picks them up. As a result of this system, the message is being reinforced that it is really acceptable for the other spouse to leave the dirty clothes there on the floor. He or she is rewarded for putting dirty clothes on the floor, and the only penalty is listening to a complaint before the clothes are picked up.

Suppose the system changes, and the person complaining and picking up the clothes and towels begins to change. That person decides he or she has rewarded the other's negative behavior long enough. Soon there are unsightly piles of clothes and towels on the floor, and the other spouse begins to run out of clean clothes to wear.

Now the person who has the unwanted behavior of keeping dirty clothes on the floor experiences pain instead of a mere complaint. The pain of not having clean clothes now motivates the untidy spouse to pick up after himself or herself.

If the tidy spouse can be consistent in not picking up after the messy spouse, a new system will evolve. Soon there will be two people who pick up their clothes, and there is an end to the complaining.

This is just one example of how one person in a marriage can change a system. You have the power to change a marital system. Stop and think of some of the various systems you have in your marriage: the system to communicate or not communicate anger, systems regarding groceries, cooking, chores, money, sex, and entertainment. You have many systems in your marriage. As an influencer in the system, when you change personally, additional change is possible and probable in the future of your marriage.

That is why the love agreements work. As you commit to a consistent path of change, you influence your spouse. That person now has to adapt to your new way of dealing with him or her.

Keep notes along your journey of your love agreements. You will be amazed at how you actually change your marriage with your love agreements.

Not all couples have such different levels of commitment, endurance, and motivation to change. Some couples are equally motivated, committed, and willing to endure the process of change. Both individuals are like sprinters waiting to hear the gun go off so they can run together in this race called marriage.

If this describes the attitudes of you and your spouse, you are doubly blessed. The love agreements can have a more significant impact as well as a more immediate impact. It's great when Christians compete to be more loving. I personally am really competitive. I love when I win at out-loving my wife. It's great; I can place my head on the pillow and look up to "Father-in-law" God and smile, knowing that I "won" that particular day.

But Lisa is also competitive, and I can tell when she's being more loving than me. Yes, there are days when she wins. But in the game of the love agreements, everyone wins.

So if you are one of those motivated couples, I applaud you. You both have a lot to look forward to. Some couples focus on the same love agreement at the same time, while others attack what they feel they want to attack to start and focus on different love agreements. Either way, if both people are trying to be more like Jesus by keeping their love agreements, I think that the Father and Father-in-law in heaven could be nothing but pleased.

We will discuss each of the seven love agreements in future chapters. Each agreement has a specific focus for the heart that chooses to make these agreements. But before we go into specifics about each love agreement, in the next chapter we will discuss what I call, "Let's Pretend."

As we consistently change behavior,

our behavior becomes habit.

As these habits develop,

our character changes.

Chapter Two

Let's Pretend

I remember sitting in my office with a male client who was going on about how difficult his marriage had become. After listening for a while, a question popped into my head. I thought about the question for a minute and decided that it would be a great way to guide this client into a more positive direction.

So during his next pause, I said, "Joe, let me ask you something." He looked at me as if to say, *What? A counselor who asks questions?* I looked him straight in the eye, man-to-man style, and asked, "When was your marriage really good?"

You could see the wheels in Joe's head come to a screeching halt. He was really on a roll with his negativity. Hit like a bull's-eye, Joe paused. Silently I waited as he started to look up to the ceiling as he was searching his memory over the last twenty years of marriage.

He smiled and then grinned as to say, "I got you, doc." Then he said, "You know, about three years ago was the best my marriage has ever been."

"What happened three years ago?" I asked, curious to hear what lay behind the smirk of this burly man.

Laughingly he replied, "Well, three years ago I bought a book."

"You bought a book?" I asked. You could tell Joe was enjoying this conversation more than I was because he knew the end of the story.

"Yes, I bought one of those marriage books. You know, kind of like the type *you* write."

I said, "Really?"

"Yes," he replied, "and I actually did everything it told me to do. I complimented my wife; I helped around the house, asked about her day, and even gave her time away from the kids."

I asked, "And what was the result?"

"It was great, doc. It was the best seven months of our marriage. My wife actually told me that she loved me. She would initiate sex, and we actually looked forward to having time together."

"So, what happened?" I asked.

It was as if he was baiting his story for the punch line, which only he knew. Then he blurted out: "I stopped doing those things."

"You stopped?" I asked with amazement on my face.

"Yeah, and it's been downhill ever since," Joe said sullenly.

Joe is a great example of how things work and change over time in a relationship. Joe didn't get saved, find a new philosophical core belief, or memorize some mantra daily. He simply changed his behavior for a time.

Now, to Joe's credit, for a while he did it consistently. It's almost as if he was going to see if the book he bought would actually work. He didn't even have the best of motives when he changed his behavior for the betterment of his wife. This behavioral change, even without a wholehearted heart change, produced measurable changes in his wife and improved the quality of their relationship.

Love agreements promote the development of behaviors. Over time, and with consistency, *these behaviors foster good relationships.* Just like Joe, anybody can change his or her agreements and behaviors.

You alone have the power inside of your heart to make a new love agreement. Once you make the agreement, then you can harness the power of your soul. This new agreement commands your mind, will, and emotions to follow.

Making a love agreement isn't magical. *Just making an agreement does not immediately cause instant change.* We have to go one step further than just a positive confession; *we must take action.*

You see, as we take action the process starts. Your behavior begins to change the system of how things are usually done in your marriage.

I remember Carl and Karla, a relatively young couple who were having great difficulty in their communication system. When either of them would start a conflict or a perceived conflict, the other would up the ante in the volume of his or her comments. The other one would also increase the number of cutting remarks made. Before you knew it, this otherwise good Christian couple would begin screaming curse words at the top of their lungs. They could go for more than an hour like this.

Of course, they would eventually kiss and make up, but what a mess they made of their relationship. They came to counseling looking for help discovering all the deep-seated issues they thought must be lurking within. Although there probably were some internal issues to deal with, we took the behavioral route to change. I asked them to go home, make a stop sign, and place it on the refrigerator.

We established a rule that either partner could grab that stop sign and place it near the face of the other person. This initiated an immediate five-minute time-out. During this time, neither spouse could say a word to the other until the timer in the kitchen went off. If they started to fight again, the stop sign could be used again.

This couple followed the directions to a T, and within a few weeks they were able to get control of the escalating verbal abuse they were inflicting on each other previously. The secret to this couple's success wasn't just the stop sign. It was the consistency in which this couple utilized it.

Their consistency created a habit over a few weeks. Day after day, and sometimes several times in a couple of hours, the stop sign created silence. Getting control of their volume and of their cutting remarks was achieved because of their consistent behavior.

This couple consistently applied a simple behavior, and because they did, something else happened: their characters were changing. They were moving from an out-of-control character to one with greater self-control.

So it is with all of us. *As we consistently change behavior, our behavior becomes habit. As these habits develop, our character changes.* That is the ultimate goal of these love agreements. They are made so that we can have greater characters. As Christians, we are encouraged to develop our characters. The love agreements are one tool that can help or improve our characters. One person with a better character can change the way a marriage operates.

LET'S PRETEND

C. S. Lewis said that we acquire new behaviors by playing the children's game "Let's Pretend." That is, the only way to acquire a habit of good behavior is to pretend that we already have the behavior trait and to perform the actions that define it. For example, if we want to be more patient, we must pretend to be patient and do things that a patient person does.

I think C. S. Lewis is on to something here. I especially like the idea of thinking of improving our characters through a game. It is much easier to consider playing a game than it is to tackle developing our characters.

I enjoy making games out of tasks. It makes the task so much more fun. Also, for me, it brings a little competition into the activity. The game aspect makes me look for an opportunity to practice a particular behavior.

I was a frequent guest on a particular Christian television talk show, and, over time, the host and I became friends. One day she told me about a game she and the crew created. The game was simple. The crew would come up with a word, any word, and the host was challenged to use that word sometime during her hour of interviewing her guests.

So unbeknownst to the other guest, if the host said this agreed-upon word, then the host would win. If she couldn't get the word worked into the interview, the crew would win. I think the prize for winning was bragging rights for the day or an occasional Coca-Cola. This little game would go on day after day without anyone in the audience ever knowing what was going on.

That's the game part of having a love agreement. You can play the game by yourself, and your spouse will never know. Just like the host of the television program, you can rack up wins or losses, and the audience will never know a game is happening.

In *Intimacy: A 100-Day Guide to Lasting Relationships*, I wrote about what I called the "holiest of competitions."[1] I suggested that one person in the marriage make a game of out-loving his or her spouse. Those who played the game were winners.

When I play the game, Lisa doesn't know, but I know what I am trying to accomplish. Honestly, just playing the game makes it fun for me throughout the day. I still feel good even though I do not act perfectly, which none of us can do. At the end of one of these "game days," I know there have been times during the day when

I have behaved better than usual, and I feel good just for having played the game.

So as you travel through the rest of the pages of this book, keep in mind that by introducing you to these seven love agreements, I am giving you an opportunity to participate in seven different games. Each game focuses on one of the seven love agreements.

Oh, I can hear the comments now: "You mean I don't need to get deep therapy and spend thousands of dollars?" "I don't have to spend hours reading all about marriage?" "I don't have to fast and pray to get all my character defects removed so that I can have a better marriage?"

I am 100 percent in favor of you committing to do the work necessary to deal with any of the things you may need to do to heal and get free from the past. Getting free of the pain of the past is what will allow you to have a better present and future. The love agreements are just another way to go about it. You'll be able to see the results for playing the game of "Let's Pretend" with the love agreements.

THE GAME

According to C. S. Lewis, the game was relatively simple. In your mind you would choose a certain virtue you would like to grow in. Once you picked the virtue, you would pretend to be a person who already had this characteristic.

Suppose you wanted to acquire the virtue of listening—a great virtue to possess in any relationship, but even more critical in a marriage relationship.

So let's suppose that Brittany, who is married to Chase, decides to play the game. She starts to really listen to Chase when he speaks to her. She sets some simple goals for herself at first.

Her first goals for playing the game are:

1. Wait until Chase has completed his sentence before I speak.

2. Ask if he has anything more to say about a topic before I talk to him about it.

Brittany keeps a small piece of paper and a pen in her purse. She acts as if she already has the virtue of listening. She and Chase have many conversations throughout the week and many more on the weekend.

After each conversation, she marks on the piece of paper in her purse if "Yes, I listened" or "No, I didn't." She reviews her paper daily to see if she is improving on the virtue, and over time she sees that her listening is improving. Her interruptions and assumptions of what he is saying decrease significantly.

Now Brittany can take the game to a whole new level. Over the last two months, she has mastered the first two goals. Now she sets the goals slightly higher, because she wants to do more than just listen—*she wants to become a great listener.* Now her goals are:

1. To reflect back some of what Chase is saying so I can clearly understand his thoughts: "What I am hearing you say is . . ." or "Do I understand that you're saying . . . ?"

2. To listen to what he is feeling as well as to what he is saying.

Again she repeats the pattern of keeping track of her progress. As the weeks go by, Brittany not only becomes a better listener to Chase; she becomes a better listener to almost everyone.

She has trained herself to hear people. She acted as if she was listening. Over time her behavior became a habit. The habit became her character.

As a result, Brittany's new virtue impacts her marriage tremendously. She notices that the once aloof and quiet Chase is talking a whole lot more to her, *and talking about much more meaningful things.* To Brittany's surprise, Chase also started, unknowingly, becoming a great listener himself.

Brittany has learned what many others who play "Let's Pretend" have learned. *It works!* First trying on a new virtue feels a little unfamiliar, uncomfortable, or even odd. As time and consistent behavior continue, the playing becomes real. With a little more time, what once felt unfamiliar becomes as comfortable as last year's winter sweater. And, like that sweater, the virtue looks good on you.

BEARING FRUIT

Playing the game of "Let's Pretend" with the love agreements is a way to bear spiritual fruit in your life. This is not simply a matter of exercising willpower. The Holy Spirit in you will help you choose and do the right things, and the Lord Himself will work the pattern of behavior into your character.

There is *accidental* fruit bearing and *intentional* fruit bearing. *Accidental fruit bearing* is exactly that: an accident. It's when my wife does something, and I accidentally don't make a big deal out of it. She accidentally experiences the fruit of patience from me. She tastes the fruit, and it is good. But the next time something happens, she is more likely to taste my flesh. As an example, I may ask questions and shame her for not knowing the obvious. That fruit doesn't taste very good, and neither one of us feels good after this interaction. That's because the fruit of patience was just an accident to begin with.

Then there is *intentional fruit*. This is where you train yourself to listen and obey the Holy Spirit. That is exactly what farmers do—they harvest intentional fruit.

For instance, a farmer determines to grow corn. He doesn't just sit around waiting until corn seeds happen to fall on his hundred acres of soil. He doesn't just hope that nature will do all the work of fertilizing or watering his crop. A farmer who relies on accidental fruit is truly not a farmer.

The intentional farmer is truly the only kind of farmer. First, the farmer decides what kind of seed he wants to plant. Our corn farmer chooses corn, not barley or wheat. The farmer knows that choosing a seed doesn't bring a crop, so he is prepared to do a little thing called *work* to make that harvest of corn happen.

Day after day he gets up early (changing of behavior). He plants, waters, and fertilizes on a regular basis to get the results.

This means he not only changed his behavior, say from sleeping to planting, but also he was consistent over a season. After a while, the seed grew in an intentional manner. All you have to do is fly a plane over Kansas or some other agricultural area to see just how intentional farmers really are.

As in the natural, so it is in the spiritual. If we want to have spiritual fruit, we must learn to be intentional. The Scriptures describe this process of growing the fruit of the Spirit. (See Galatians 5:22–23.) We can be the kind of Christians who have an occasional fruit for someone to eat, or we can be someone who has intentional fruits.

You may know of a bitter, elderly person who complains constantly. This person goes to church, reads the Bible, but doesn't have a friend in the world or a family member who enjoys his or her company. This person lives a lonely life. One day a Girl Scout comes by selling cookies. For whatever reason, this elderly person behaves very graciously and is kind to the little girl. He or she even gives the Girl Scout an extra dollar tip, because she is such a good little Girl Scout.

Unfortunately, for many people, harvesting occasional fruit like this is the norm. You don't want to be that elderly person with barely any fruit to offer to others in the barren land we call earth.

Now, dream with me for a minute. Imagine a life of fruitfulness, a life that gets more fruitful with every passing day. Because you are growing intentional fruit, the fruit of the Spirit flowing out of your life feed those around you regularly. Your wife is overflowing with your patience and kindness. Your husband has a strong foundation because of the diet of praise he has received from the fruits of your tree.

Your children are filled with self-esteem because of all the nurturing they receive from your fruitfulness. You yourself are satiated and strong because of the fruit you get to eat of your spouse's tree. Then there's that additional fruit you receive from your children. Wow, you are full and satiated.

Now, don't stop dreaming. Go a little further down the road. You plowed a field of intentional fruit. Your spouse and children are not only blessed by the fruit, but they are also blessed because you have taught them how to be intentional in growing the fruit of the Spirit. Now the harvest is growing multigenerationally. Your children's children have the fruit of the Spirit to give to their generation. Not only are they saved, but they also have fruit.

This is the dream I hope to help your heart grab hold of through an understanding of the love agreements. In the pages ahead, you will walk through the seven love agreements. The agreements are powerful tools for teaching you how to grow fruit practically. This fruit is the fruit that God wants you to have on your trees.

But remember this: fruit is not grown for the benefit of the trees. The tree never eats its own fruit. The tree simply grows the fruit to give away. There are no direct benefits to the tree for growing fruit except perhaps the sheer pleasure of being what God created it to be. The tree doesn't control what others do with the fruit.

One person who receives an apple from the tree may spit it out.

He may prefer diving into his candy bar and soda. Another person receiving a fruit may just pass by the sweetness, expecting that it will taste like every other apple she has eaten. But occasionally there will be the people who receive the apple and are truly grateful for it. They savor the sweetness; they make the sounds of satiation as they eat the pleasured fruit. They fully experience the fruit.

In just the same way, you don't get to control how your spouse or others respond to your fruit. They may disdain your fruit, not even noticing it. Or they may savor your new fruitfulness. It is simply your job to be fruitful. The first command God gave mankind was to be fruitful and multiply. (See Genesis 1:28.)

Fruitfulness involves more than merely growing physical fruit. God, in Christ through the Holy Spirit, planted His very nature inside of you. This river of life flows deep inside. It is similar to a stream that runs under dry ground. As you dig deeper, you get to the stream. You cultivate this by building a well to bring the water below ground to the surface so people can drink this life-giving water.

The Spirit of God has already been planted within you. Now it's your job to cultivate the seed of His nature. It is not going to be an easy thing to do all the time. There's a layer of dirt through which the farmer's corn seeds must push to reach the sunlight. That dirt outweighs that little seed, and it will have to struggle hard to break through. In the same manner, God's Spirit has to push through the dirt we call *our flesh.*

Our flesh may be innately selfish, rude, and indulgent. The Spirit of God inside of us is none of these things. Thus, there is a conflict. The Spirit wants to push through these layers of dirt so it can be seen and tasted by others through you.

If you are aware of this process, you will feel the discomfort of this conflict between the seed of the Spirit and the dirt of the flesh. During this process you will have some choices to make.

You can just throw more dirt on the seed and make the seed work harder. You can choose to ignore the seed and have occasional and accidental fruitfulness.

Or you can acknowledge the seed of God's very own nature already in you. You can take time on a regular basis to nurture its growth by watering it, giving it light, and trying to remove some of the layers of dirt to make a shorter path for the seed to grow through so it can be seen and eaten by others, too.

As for me, I want the shorter path. I want God to be glorified by allowing more of His kind, loving, gentle nature to be seen through me. I want people all over to be able to taste the fruit of God. I want them to see Jesus. I am aware that I fail occasionally, just like everyone else. But over time and with cultivation, I want the success of His fruit to be dominant in my life.

I know I am not the only one who has a desire for His seed to be seen and eaten by others. Probably that is also the desire of your heart. "How do you know?" you ask. I know because that is the desire of the seed, the desire of God's Spirit within you. You, by the Spirit of God, have His fruit inside of you. God, through Christ and by the Holy Spirit, has already planted His seed in you.

Just as a seed in the natural realm contains the nature of the fruit it will become, so, too, within that seed of the Spirit planted in you is the very DNA of God: His heart, His mind, His will, and His nature.

You see, the seed of God in you is already faithful. The seed inside of you is patient and forgiving. The seed in you also desires to be of service, to be respectful, to be kind, and express itself in celebration.

In the seven love agreements, we are acknowledging a seed that already rests inside of your being. In the following pages I want to help you understand how to nurture seven different aspects of this seed. My heart's desire is that you become so fruitful that not only your spouse benefit, but also those around you benefit from your fruitfulness.

So come along, we have a lot of intentional farming to do. Oh, yes, it's work. And yes, it's daily. Some parts of the field will be easy to plow, and some will be harder.

I caution you here, don't focus on the work. Jesus went to the cross (works) because of the joy that was set before Him. He could look down the halls of time and see that you were so worth it.

He was beaten, but it still was worth it to touch your soul and be in a relationship with you in the distant future. So don't worry; it won't get that bad for you, but there will be some discomfort here and there as the dirt turns over to expose the seed in the ground.

But look at the season of fruit. Imagine your marriage with the increased fruit of God in it. Imagine yourself with more fruit to offer. Imagine your children living fruitful lives. Now go down a few generations; look down from heaven to see your great-great-grandchild giving fruit away like candy to his or her generation. Feel the hand on your shoulder and see His smile as Jesus speaks to you and says, "Well done."

Oh, the joy that is set before you is eternal. So get ready to plow; there is a harvest so sweet ahead of you.

$\mathcal{L}$OVE $\mathcal{A}$GREEMENT #1

I will be faithful to my spouse at all times

and in all circumstances.

Chapter Three

Love Agreement #1:
FAITHFULNESS

aithfulness is the first love agreement you will make and is the cornerstone upon which the other love agreements can be built and can thrive. Without the agreement of faithfulness, your marriage will suffer seasons of damage. In my seventeen years as a counselor, I have seen the ravages of unfaithfulness in various areas of many couples' marriages.

For many Christians, faithfulness is considered to be almost a given. If a Christian couple walks down the aisle and makes a vow in the sight of God, church, and community, most believe, of course, that both individuals are going to keep their word.

I wish this was true. Yet, many Bible-believing, church-attending Christians fail to keep their vow of faithfulness. One day last year, Lisa was reading an issue of *Charisma* magazine. Lisa is a voracious reader of all kinds of material. As is her habit, she clips out and highlights anything she feels is important for me to know. On this day, she leaned over to me with her *Charisma* magazine and said, "Look at this; this is hard to believe." She had my interest because her big, beautiful green eyes had just gotten a whole lot bigger. So I looked at what she was reading. The article was citing some research stating that Christians are out-divorcing the world by a couple of percentage points. It was hard to believe that 50 percent of all secular marriages end in divorce. Yet even harder to believe was the fact that Christian marriages were beating those numbers by a couple of percentage points. I put the *Charisma* magazine down in my lap and paused.

This truly is a sad statement. Christians today have the Spirit of God, the Word of God, great churches and pastors, marriage ministries, marriage conferences, marriage counselors, and more books on marriage than at any other time in the history of the church. Yet they are failing at marriage.

It's even sadder when you look back fifty to one hundred years ago and see that more people in the church were staying married. Remember, that was before marriage ministries, in general, existed. Even though marriage counseling and conferences were scant in the Christian world, more people were staying married.

What is the reason? One reason is because the generations before us understood the agreement of faithfulness. They took the covenant of marriage very seriously. They were taught the biblical meaning of covenant. Today, many have lost sight of the simple meaning of covenant. In biblical times, when a couple was being married, as a part of the marriage ceremony they would cut an animal in half, allowing the blood and insides of the animal to scatter all over the place, exposed to both individuals. Then they would walk between the animal and make their agreement, saying to each other, "If I do not keep my agreement, may worse than what happened to this animal happen to me." Now that's an agreement to be faithful.

I remember when Lisa and I were engaged. We took our engagement very seriously. We read every book and listened to every tape on marriage preparation and marriage we could get our hands on. Lisa and I walked down the aisle and said our vows of "until death do us part." We are absolutely serious about this. In our hearts, divorce is not an option. We are committed to going through the various stages of life, dealing with the issues, and feeling the pain and joys of a life *together.*

I often kid Lisa that I am asking Jesus to allow me to have her as my wife during those thousand years when Christ is on earth. I really love Lisa, and I am committed to her for life, and she is to me.

TYPES OF FAITHFULNESS

Before we move on to our agreement of faithfulness, I thought it would be a great idea to discuss the various types of faithfulness to your spouse to which you commit for life.

Spiritual faithfulness

Spiritual faithfulness is a crucial form of faithfulness in a Christian marriage. Spiritual faithfulness means putting God first in absolute loyalty. This means that you as an individual will develop and maintain the spiritual muscle of faithfulness through prayer, study, fellowship, and service. We express faithfulness to God individually by aspiring to know, love, and serve Him only in greater and greater measure throughout our lifetime.

As individuals, we are faithful to God. This is the first and probably most critical aspect of faithfulness. If we don't maintain an individual relationship with our Lord and Savior Jesus Christ, we weaken the very foundation of our marriage.

Spiritual faithfulness also means that we agree to grow together toward Christ. We are committed to the principle of seeking God together.

I want to take a moment and expose you to a great idea that has been very helpful to couples who attend our Intimacy conferences, which we conduct around the country. Most of you have accepted God as Father. Jesus' teachings about God often use the analogy of God as a father. I don't think anyone who is a Christian would argue that God is our Father.

Yet I want to take this a step further. God is not just your Father; He is also your *Father-in-law*, because He is also the Father of your spouse. Hence, He is your all-knowing, omnipresent Father-in-law. He sees how you treat your spouse and how you talk about your spouse to yourself and others.

For most couples who marry, I am sure that both individuals maintain a relationship with their natural in-laws. For some this may include a few holidays a year, occasional phone calls, visits, or vacations together.

Could you imagine, under normal circumstances, marrying your spouse and never seeing your in-laws again? That would seem odd, at best, and very rude, at worst. Yet that is exactly what some Christians do with God. It's as if they say, "Thanks for the spouse." Yet they never bring their spouses back to their Father-in-law God. They don't pray together, and they rarely discuss God's will or His Word. Oh, they don't mind going to church, but privately they never go visit the Father-in-law, who not only gave them their Christian spouse but also specially made that special person just for him or her.

Part of spiritual faithfulness is being faithful to spending spiritual time together. This includes praying together, having times of worship together, getting in the Word, having spiritual conversations, and seeking God's will for each other and for family. The love agreement of faithfulness is definitely one that includes spiritual faithfulness.

It's possible that you may have an unsaved or difficult spouse. For you, maintain your own spiritual faithfulness.

At a Winning at Marriage conference where I spoke, there was a time when we had couples pray together. The next day a man shared a testimony saying that when he and his wife prayed together the day before, it was the first prayer they had prayed together in twenty years. This was really a testimony of faithfulness to God and of God eventually breaking through to bring them to a new level of spiritual faithfulness.

Emotional faithfulness

Emotional faithfulness is also an important part of marital faithfulness. Emotional faithfulness means that your spouse is the person with whom you really share your heart or emotional self. Your spouse should not be second to your parents, friends, co-workers, or even to your children.

Emotional faithfulness means putting your spouse first in your relationships with absolute loyalty. Your spouse is the person you allow to see you at the core of your being.

As a Christian counselor, I realize that you may have little to no training in understanding emotions. If so, I strongly recommend my book *Intimacy: A 100-Day Guide to Lasting Relationships*. In this book, I outline a feeling exercise you can do to identify and communicate your feelings with each other.[1] It takes about ninety days to achieve a good skill level in emotions.

Once you have this skill, it will be much easier to maintain and grow in emotional faithfulness with your spouse. I am so glad that I can share my heart and feelings with Lisa on a daily basis. Because of this consistent behavior, she is the safest person on earth to me.

Sexual faithfulness

Sexual faithfulness is probably the first idea of faithfulness that popped into your head when we started this conversation on faithfulness. *Faithfulness requires exclusive devotion to each other.*

You express faithfulness to your spouse by preserving the sexual exclusiveness of your relationship. Sexual faithfulness must be maintained as a top priority in your relationship.

As a counselor who has worked with sexually addicted men for more than seventeen years, I have never met a man who did not regret his choice to commit adultery. Sexual faithfulness is more than just not having physical sex with another person. Sexual faithfulness means your spouse is the only person with whom you are sexual—*including yourself.*

Self-sex is self-destructive in most cases. It takes the chemical bonding of husband and wife and attaches it to fantasy or pornography. Pornography must be eliminated completely. I speak at Sex, Men, and God conferences around the world and throughout America. I go into Catholic, Presbyterian, Methodist, Baptist, and almost every form of nondenominational church there is. Regardless of denomination, when I ask for a show of hands as to who believes they are struggling with sexual addiction, 50 percent of the men at my conferences raise their hands.

I believe that if wives asked their husbands two questions, men would be more willing to open up and get further help for their problem. These two questions are:

- "When was the last time you looked at pornography?"
- "When was the last time you masturbated?"

I've noticed that when men start answering these questions honestly, they begin to heal.

Blocking the Internet is very critical to sexual faithfulness. At www.intimatematters.com we have a porn blocker available for visitors, as well as free newsletters and materials for those who struggle in this area. One option with this porn blocker is that you can set it up so that every stroke you make on the computer can be e-mailed to an accountability person. Your accountability person can now be aware of what you are viewing on the Internet.

We live in a very sexually sick culture. We must be wise. Sexual faithfulness also includes not flirting or giving sexual energy to other people. *We maintain sexual faithfulness by avoiding even a hint of interaction or flirtation with another person.*

Sexual faithfulness is one of the great agreements to keep. Couples who have made this agreement—and kept it—do not have the damage and pain in their marriage relationship that other couples have. If there is a lack of sexual faithfulness in a relationship, it takes time to regain resiliency and trust. If you are struggling with sexual faithfulness, I encourage you to get immediate help and information. We all need to make an agreement from now forward to walk in sexual faithfulness.

Financial faithfulness

Financial faithfulness is also important in a marriage relationship. Everyone has heard about the two things that people argue about most in a marriage: *sex and money.* That may be true for most couples, but it doesn't have to be in your marriage relationship.

It takes a financial plan to create financial faithfulness. It involves more than a budget; it's a life plan. Your financial plan includes budget, retirement, college funds, and creating the wealth you perceive God has given you permission to create.

Your plan will include a commitment to tithing. I could write a whole book on the blessings and curses of tithing, but I won't. I can just tell you that nearly every couple I have met who were having financial struggles were couples who were not tithing. On the other side of the fulcrum, I can also tell you that the richest people I have met around the country consistently give much more than 10 percent of their income to advancing the kingdom of God. Being financially faithful to God is one way to be financially faithful to each other.

As a couple, be in agreement on your spending. Without a doubt, one of you will probably want to spend more, and the other one will save more; that's God's way of balancing both of you.

Look at your philosophy of debt—your actual debt load and your agreement. It is also helpful for you to agree on the amount of independent spending each of you will do without discussing your purchase with the other spouse.

Financial faithfulness can help to provide a service of safety and teamwork that will keep your marriage strong. Maturity in this area of faithfulness will add decades of blessings into your marital life.

Parental faithfulness

Most married couples have children eventually, and it is best when both parents are involved in the nurturing and growth of their children in the ways of the Lord. As a parent, you can do your part in being a godly father or godly mother, but you cannot control your spouse's lack of responsibility or over-responsibility.

It is in your power, however, to be a team player. You can help with homework, drive the children to events, and do projects with them. But they need more than your involvement in their activities—they need to be able to sense your faithfulness to them, and preferably sense it from both parents.

Discipline and discipleship are best done by both parents consistently. When you include faithfulness in your parenting, it can make a world of difference in your family life during the years of your marriage when active parenting is involved.

Relationship faithfulness

Marriage is a great relationship—probably the greatest next to our relationship with Jesus. Marriage, however, is not the only relationship a person needs to stay stable and healthy.

We all need friends. God made us so that we do much better in life if we have friends. It is great to have friends who love you even when they can see your weaknesses. They can laugh you into seeing your faults, can be there when you are in pain, and are always available when you need a little extra help with life.

I love having friends. I am also glad Lisa has friends. After spending time with her friends, she always returns home happier for just getting together with them. They talk and can call each other for prayer.

You can only be responsible for your own relational faithfulness. Maintain some same-gender close relationships. It's wonderful when you see their phone number on your cell phone and know it's them. You're going to need friends, and they are going to need you. Help your spouse to develop his or her own friendships. You can't force your spouse to have friends, but if you offer to take care of the children at night so that he or she has some time for relationships, it can encourage him or her to have friends.

Agree to have some couple friends. This can be a great blessing for a marriage. It will be fun for each of you, and it will be great for your children to see the two of you having fun with other couples.

My Commitment to Faithfulness

Before we go any further, let's pause and actually make your faithfulness agreement in an official manner. First, I find it personally and professionally helpful to admit to any lack of agreement in an area before you make a new one. Once you acknowledge your lack, the way is clear for your heart to accept making a new agreement and to command your mind, will, and emotions to follow this new agreement.

LOVE AGREEMENT #1

I WILL BE FAITHFUL TO MY SPOUSE AT ALL TIMES
AND IN ALL CIRCUMSTANCES.

OK, it's time to go to the Lord. Please use the following prayer as a guide to break away from any lack of faithfulness that you have displayed or harbored in your relationship with your spouse.

Lord Jesus, I ask You to forgive me of the sin of unfaithfulness in any spiritual, emotional, sexual, financial, parental, or relational aspects of myself. I ask You to forgive me of the impact that any unfaithfulness in these areas has had on my spouse. I break any previous agreements to thoughts, feelings, or willfulness in my life. I command any spirit, soul, or body influences that have been in agreement with these areas of unfaithfulness to leave in the name of Jesus.

Now that you have broken your agreements to unfaithfulness, it is time to make a new agreement. This agreement is something you speak aloud. Command your heart to make a new agreement so that your mind, will, and emotions can begin to place these resources in a new direction.

SPIRITUAL FAITHFULNESS

I am officially making an agreement to spiritual faithfulness. I command my mind, will, and emotions to create new ideas, feelings, and behaviors to make this agreement. I am committed to spiritual faithfulness to Christ regardless of my spouse's own personal spiritual walk. I commit to seek God through prayer, worship, His Word, and fellowship to be spiritually faithful all the days of my life.

My spiritual faithfulness goals

In this section we outline practical, behavioral, and measurable goals for you to use to improve your spiritual faithfulness.

Underline each of the following goals you are willing to make a commitment to keep, and for each goal you underline, fill in the specific behavior you will use to reach that goal:

1. My goal is to pray daily.

2. My goal is to ask my spouse to pray with me daily.

3. My goal is to pray with my children daily.

4. My goal is to pray over the phone and in person with an accountability person.

5. My goal is to read the Bible daily.

6. My goal is to read the Bible with my spouse daily.

7. My goal is to read the Bible with my children daily.

_____

8. My goal is to have at least one spiritual conversation with someone daily.

_____

9. My goal is to spend some time just worshiping Jesus and not asking for anything.

_____

10. My goal is to invite my spouse into a time of worship together on a regular basis.

_____

11. My goal is to invite my children into a time of worship.

_____

12. My goal is to speak a verbal blessing over my spouse.

_____

13. My goal is to speak a verbal blessing over my children.

_____

EMOTIONAL FAITHFULNESS

I am officially making an agreement to emotional faithfulness. I command my mind, will, and emotions to create new ideas, feelings, and behaviors to fulfill this agreement to emotional faithfulness. I am committed to honesty in my emotions with my God, my spouse, and myself. I commit to learn and develop emotional faithfulness to my spouse as much as I possibly can all the days of my life.

My emotional faithfulness goals

Let's look at some possible ideas that are practical, behavioral, and measurable. Emotional faithfulness can be uncomfortable work for some, but I think almost anyone can improve in the area of emotional honesty.

Underline each of the following goals you are willing to make a commitment to keep, and for each goal you underline, fill in the specific behavior you will use to reach that goal.

1. My goal is to learn to identify and communicate my feelings by each day writing down two feelings along with when I first remember feeling that feeling.

    _____

2. My goal is to intentionally share two feelings from my day with my spouse.

    _____

3. My goal is to listen better to my spouse's feelings by asking him/her, "So how did you feel about that?"

_____

5. My goal is that by the end of the day I am going to write down two feelings my spouse has shared with me.

_____

6. My goal is to share at least one feeling a day with my children.

_____

7. My goal is to listen to at least one feeling a day from my children.

_____

8. My goal is to keep notes as I read the Bible and see if I can hypothesize how the various characters might have felt.

_____

Sexual Faithfulness

I am officially making an agreement to sexual faithfulness. I command my mind, will, and emotions to create new ideas, feelings, and behaviors to fulfill this agreement to sexual faithfulness. I am committed to sexual purity to my God, my spouse, and myself. I am committed to remove or stop behaviors or beliefs that are confusing to sexual faithfulness. I am committed to sexual purity in every aspect, emotionally or behaviorally, all the days of my life.

My sexual faithfulness goals

Sexual faithfulness is critical to the strength of a marriage. Here in this area of marriage it is crucial to have practical, behavioral, and measurable goals to be successful. Here are some ideas for you to maintain sexual faithfulness.

Underline each of the following goals you are willing to make a commitment to keep, and for each goal you underline, fill in the specific behavior you will use to reach that goal.

1. My goal is to limit entertainment that portrays fornication or adultery.

   _____

2. My goal is to limit entertainment that discusses sexuality regularly.

   _____

3. My goal is to avoid all pornography.

   _____

4. My goal is to install a porn blocker with accountability features on my home and office computers.

    _____

5. My goal is to answer honestly or ask questions regarding self-behavior or pornography.

    _____

6. My goal is to maintain a connection with my spouse when in public.

    _____

7. My goal is to talk about my spouse when meeting people of the opposite sex.

    _____

8. My goal is not to participate in any flirting or sexual humor with anyone.

    _____

9. My goal is to avoid people who seem too interested in me or who give off sexual energy.

    _____

10. My goal is not to talk about weaknesses in my marriage except with my spouse or someone mutually agreed upon.

_____

11. My goal is to be a giving lover to my spouse.

_____

12 My goal is to nurture my spouse during sexual encounters.

_____

13. My goal is to regularly communicate with my spouse about how happy I am with our sex life.

_____

14. My goal is to be creative in the way my spouse would appreciate sexual creativity.

_____

15. My goal is to be proactive in solving sexual issues. (I recommend the book *Intimacy: A 100-Day Guide to Lasting Relationships* for these discussions.)

_____

16. My goal is to be proactive with age-appropriate sexual information to my children.

FINANCIAL FAITHFULNESS

I am officially making an agreement to financial faithfulness. I command my mind, will, and emotions to create new ideas, feelings, and behavior to fulfill this agreement to financial faithfulness. I am committed to financial faithfulness to my God, my spouse, and myself. I am committed to stop behaviors or beliefs that are contrary to financial faithfulness. I am committed to financial faithfulness in every aspect, emotionally or behaviorally, all the days of my life.

My financial faithfulness goals

Because finances are one of the areas couples can have tension, this is a great area to have practical, behavioral, and measurable goals. Here are a few ideas for you to consider.

Underline each of the following goals you are willing to make a commitment to keep, and for each goal you underline, fill in the specific behavior you will use to reach that goal.

1. My goal is to meet with a financial planner to cover issues of retirement, college funds, and asset management.

---

2. My goal is to tithe.

_____

3. My goal is to evaluate debt and our philosophy of debt.

_____

4. My goal is to discuss money matters with my spouse monthly.

_____

5. My goal is to evaluate monthly spending patterns.

_____

6. My goal is to have an agreement I will not spend without discussing it with my spouse.

_____

7. My goal is not to participate in unilateral large purchases.

_____

8. My goal is to have an annual review of our financial plan.

_____

PARENTAL FAITHFULNESS

I am officially making an agreement to parental faithfulness. I command my mind, will, and emotions to create new ideas, feelings, and behaviors to fulfill this agreement to parental faithfulness. I am committed to parental faithfulness to my God, my spouse, and myself. I am committed to stop behaviors or beliefs that are contrary to parental faithfulness. I am committed to parental faithfulness in every aspect, emotionally and behaviorally, all the days of my life.

My parental faithfulness goals

Parenting is a tough job no matter who you are. My wife, Lisa, has the gift of administration. Before she worked for me, when she left a job, it usually took two people to replace her. Yet, at times, I have seen parenting overwhelm us both. Having a plan that is practical, behavioral, and measurable can really help a marriage during the primary years of child rearing.

Underline each of the following goals you are willing to make a commitment to keep, and for each goal you underline, fill in the specific behavior you will use to reach that goal.

1. My goal is to read one parenting book per quarter.

   _____

2. My goal is to discuss agreed-upon discipline with my spouse and children.

   _____

3. My goal is to pick up the children from school ___ times per week.

_____

4. My goal is to do homework with the children ___ times per week.

_____

5. My goal is to pray with my children ___ times per week.

_____

6. My goal is to read the Bible with my children ___ times per week.

_____

7. My goal is to help with the laundry ___ times per week.

_____

8. My goal is to cook or clean up after mealtime ___ times per week.

_____

9. My goal is to give my spouse a total break from me and the children ___ times per month.

_____

10 My goal is to take each child on a "date" with me alone
____ times per month.

Relational Faithfulness

I am officially making an agreement to relational faithfulness. I command my mind, will, and emotions to create new ideas, feelings, and behaviors to fulfill this agreement to relational faithfulness. I am committed to relational faithfulness to my God, my spouse, and myself. I am committed to stop behaviors or beliefs that are contrary to relational faithfulness in every aspect, emotionally and behaviorally, all the days of my life.

My relational faithfulness goals

As stated earlier, you and I will need friends to stay individually healthy. This is an area often neglected, especially during child rearing. This area needs some practical, behavioral, and measurable goals to be successful and intentional in relationships.

Underline each of the following goals you are willing to make a commitment to keep, and for each goal you underline, fill in the specific behavior you will use to reach that goal.

1. My goal is to make a list of people of the same gender as myself who might be options for friends.

---

2. My goal is to call potential friends on my list to attempt to get together.

    _____

3. My goal is to actually get together with a friend or potential friend ___ times per month.

    _____

4. My goal is to contact friends that I have had in the past to reconnect a relationship.

    _____

5. My goal is to have a friend for specific purposes in my life (spiritual, entertainment, exercise, mutual interest).

    _____

6. My goal is to give my spouse ___ times per month to meet his/her friends.

    _____

7. My goal is to make a couple calls a week to friends.

    _____

8. My goal is to get the e-mail addresses of my friends to stay in touch.

    _____

9. My goal is to have people over to the house ___ times per year.

    _____

STAYING COMMITTED

Wow, you just made your first love agreement—and established the goals that will help you to keep your commitment to your faithfulness agreement! No doubt some of the facets of goal setting for faithfulness were harder for you to make than others. But making this love agreement of faithfulness will bring clarity to aspects of faithfulness you are already wading through.

Your new faithfulness agreement will help you to strengthen those areas of faithfulness where you were less than strong in your life.

Regardless of your experience, you and I know it takes more than a declaration to move from ideal to behavior. How many times have you made a commitment to lose a couple of pounds, and...well...it just didn't happen on schedule.

That's OK. As a counselor, I know people need a plan to follow and must be accountable to someone to be really successful in carrying out the plan. In these final sections of the chapter, I want to lay out some behavioral plans to help you to be successful in your love agreement of faithfulness.

Remember that the love agreements are *behavioral*. It's your behavior change that starts to make a difference within and then moves into the system of your marriage. Remember also that it will take more than a day or a week to see some of these changes.

The key to being successful in a love agreement is having a plan and an accountability partner of the same gender. I will suggest some ideas that have worked for me and others, which you may want to incorporate into your plan. These are merely ideas; ultimately you will establish your own plan. Your ideas will be just as good, or better, because you are more familiar with your situation than I will ever be. Let's get started!

MEASURING

Now that you have written down your behavioral plan for reaching your goals, I want you to be able to be successful within that plan. I have found with myself, and with clients, that if it's measurable, I am much more likely to be successful.

Every time—and yes, there have been several times—I am going to try to lose weight, I have two choices: immeasurable and unintentional; or measurable and intentional. You see, when I do the oh-I-really-want-to-lose-weight song and dance, if I don't do more than just that, I don't usually lose weight at all. I might even have an idea of a plan, but I don't usually follow through with whatever the plan is. My ideas are just too vague, like something about food and exercise, but the details are illusive to me.

Now when I get measurable and intentional, I get serious. I get a piece of paper out. This time I write down the categories of my goals for my plan. The categories might be:

1. Exercise each day for fifteen minutes.
2. Eliminate unnecessary sugar.
3. Do not eat after 5:00 p.m.
4. Write down my weight for each day (just for factual reality).

Then daily I measure these goals.

Now I'm kind of tricky, so I know I can fool myself. To avoid any reason for not keeping my goals, I tape my goals on my mirror where I shave. Now I have to face these goals every day. I have to check off each category of my goals. If I get lazy and don't check off my goals even when I'm failing, I know I'm not being honest about losing weight.

I remind myself continually of a phrase I have told my clients for years: "Believe behavior." You see, the one important thing that I have learned over the years is that behavior always tells the truth. Words and intentions can fool you, but one's behavior is always truth. The measurement aspect lets us see the truth about ourselves. Once we know the truth, the truth will set us free to grow.

As you walk through the love agreements, I strongly—*and I mean strongly*—recommend some form of measurement of your behavior against your goal. If you set a parental goal to do the laundry twice a week, then measure yourself. Make a chart covering one full month, and tape it to your mirror or wall for a month. Write your goal at the top of the paper, and every day record your progress. If you hit your goal of twice a week regularly, after a while you will feel good because of your progress.

This measurement process really works. I remember a while back, Lisa and I were having a conversation again about how she felt I wasn't helping enough around the house. She stated that she just wanted five minutes a day from me when I would pick up, fold laundry, or do the dishes.

Because I travel regularly speaking at conferences or as a guest on media shows, I know that when I am not at home I cannot give her much help. But I really felt that when I was at home, I was intentionally being helpful. So I decided to practice what I preach.

I went to the kitchen drawer—we all have one that has everything in it, and I reached in there and found a pad of paper and pen. I listed thirty-plus days and left a column where I could keep track of my progress each day. Then I began to keep track of when I started and stopped doing things around the house. I did this for three months. When I was home, I averaged between thirty to forty-five minutes every day of helping my wife around our house.

At the end of the three months, I asked Lisa if I needed to continue doing this for a fourth month. She told me that it wasn't necessary to keep measuring my helpful behavior. Amazingly, we haven't had that conversation ever since.

Measurement works. Years ago Lisa would repeatedly state that she thought there was something wrong with my hearing. After a while I went to get my ears tested. The factual test showed that my hearing was really good. Again, measuring the facts about my physical hearing ended an ongoing conversation.

When you measure, you operate on facts. When you don't measure behavior and facts, you're left with your feelings or the feelings of your spouse. When all you have is feelings and discussions, arguments can be ongoing for years.

So when you take on a love agreement, please measure yourself. You deserve to be in reality as you progress. This one factor of measurement will be the difference between reading another marriage book and seeing the changes you hope for.

ACCOUNTABILITY

Accountability is a dirty word to the "touchy feely" group, who just wants to "believe" in change. There are those who want to *believe* instead of *behave*. If you are one of these, this section might be difficult to process.

Accountability is one of the greatest strengths a Christian can utilize in his or her walk with the Lord. I have worked with many Christian men who struggle with sexual addiction. Sexual addiction is one of the most severe addictions a person can have. Accountability is one of the major structures that alleviates its power and can keep it in remission for a lifetime.

With accountability you can totally maximize the love agreements. We all want success in various areas of our lives. I find that accountability improves the odds of success. For many couples, accountability is the power behind marital counseling. In marital counseling, the couple attends sessions regularly and sits in front of the therapist. The therapist reviews the couple's goals and arguments. Accountability, by itself, has motivated many couples to actually follow through.

Accountability is simply bringing someone into the loop with you. You let that person know what love agreements or facets of a love agreement you are working on. You set up some times to get together or call each other to go over your goals and the facts of your behavior. This helps you tremendously to keep good records of your behavior during your love agreement process. Sometimes this can turn into an opportunity for mutual accountability, whereby both you and your accountability partner discuss your individual goals and help each other assess the progress both of you are making.

An accountability person can be almost anyone of the same gender. If the person is Christian, it is helpful because he or she will understand why you are doing what you are doing. Someone local may be better than someone far away. You will be amazed at how this can work wonders in your life as you walk through all of the love agreements.

Faithfulness is a foundational love agreement. As I discussed earlier, this agreement covers many more areas of your marriage than just fidelity. Faithfulness can become an incredible lifestyle. As you walk through the various facets of faithfulness with goals, measures, and accountability, you are likely to be very successful at becoming faithful.

LOVE AGREEMENT #2

I will not try to change things about my spouse that I do not like but will modify my behaviors that annoy my partner.

Chapter Four

Love Agreement #2:
PATIENCE

Get comfortable, find a cozy chair, and put your feet up for this love agreement on patience. We all need growth in this area. I'm pretty sure that deep down inside you know that you are not as patient as you could be—or as patient as Jesus would like you to be—with the most precious person in your life, your spouse. I know that I'm not with Lisa.

But before you begin to feel guilty and just skip this chapter, let me encourage you with this: *you can grow patience in your life!* Remember that patience is a fruit, and fruit takes time to grow. A fruit tree needs nutrients, water, and light, and for you to grow patience, you will also need the nutrients of God's Word, the water of His Spirit, and the light of honesty in your heart as He exposes your impatience. Remember that patience is just one step toward better character. (See James 1:2–4.)

Personally, I don't like the process that I have to go through when I am *unintentionally* learning patience. The unintentional process of learning patience often causes me to learn to be patient by enduring trials and periods of testing. There is a better way to learn patience. It is learning patience by means of an *intentional, measurable, and accountable process.*

Before we take a closer look at this intentional process, let me help you to understand the heart of God when it comes to marriage. Many couples are confused on the purpose of marriage. Many Americans have an especially faulty notion that the purpose of marriage is to make them happy.

If you enter marriage thinking that marriage is supposed to make you happy, both you and your spouse will be very disappointed. It isn't the purpose of marriage—or the responsibility of your spouse—to make you happy. *No, happiness is an individual responsibility.* I am responsible to be happy. If I'm not happy, that's my choice alone. Lisa, my beautiful wife, can't make me happy. I wouldn't place that burden on anyone. It would be cruel to impose that expectation upon your spouse or on someone else.

If we look at marriage from God's perspective, we will discover that God's purpose in marriage is to make you more Christlike. Here's the idea. God picks someone who is not like you, someone who is different in many different ways. Over time, through the Spirit of God, you begin to change—and so does your spouse. These changes make both of you look more like Jesus as the years go by.

The goal of marriage is to enable both of you to become more Christlike with every passing day. The love agreements are so important, because they take the focus off your attempts to change your spouse and place the focus on you becoming more like Christ.

The Holy Spirit is able to mold your character more and more into the character of Christ through the relationship you have with your spouse. The strengths and spiritual gifts that I possess are only a limited, fractional expression of God's nature. The strengths and gifts that my wife, Lisa, possesses are also just a small reflection of His completeness. But together we are more like Christ. So many times, God has enabled me to see His character and be taught to be more like Him through Lisa's expression of God.

Yet some individuals believe they are the totality of God's image, so they set a course to make their spouse into their own image. If they are organized, they set out to make their spouse organized. Being organized is a good thing, but even God is messy sometimes. He controls great storms and sometimes leaves big messes.

Early in my Christian walk I learned that when the Holy Spirit comes into your life, He is sent with this mission: kill everything that doesn't look like Christ. He is going to destroy your personality systematically and replace it with the glorious personality of His Son Jesus Christ, King of kings and Lord of heaven and earth.

So don't value your personality too much. It's just a matter of time until the Holy Spirit makes progress on your personality. Don't get too attached to your personality—be willing to take on the personality of Christ! It's a glorious day in your Christian walk when you want the personality of Christ more than you want your own. This is a great position for you to be ready to make a love agreement to patience.

There are times in every marriage relationship when your spouse is going to rub you the wrong way. This is a fact of marriage. All who are married have experienced and will experience this, probably until death.

How you deal with the annoyances of your spouse is critical. Always remember that although your spouse is imperfect, he or she is still the son or daughter of the Most High God. How you treat your spouse is very important to your relationship with God.

Let me give you a practical example. Suppose you have two children. One son's heart tends to be much more selfish, while the other son's heart tends to be more sincerely kind, loving, and unselfish. One day a situation arises where the selfish son has a great opportunity to share with his sibling two tickets to an event they would both enjoy.

But the selfish boy states that he wants to take a friend instead of his brother. This, of course, hurts the kind son, but he moves on. Later that day you find out that the kind brother gave twenty dollars to his selfish brother so he could enjoy himself at the event.

What happens instantly in your heart? Don't you want to bless the kind child immediately? You are probably still disappointed with the selfish child, which is probably the reason you didn't give him the money to spend at the event, and his kind brother did.

Remember that God is actually a parent as well. He is the parent of both you and of your spouse. He watches your interactions throughout the day. He sees who is more patient. And according to Hebrews 12:1, He is not the only one watching you; you have "so great a cloud of witnesses" watching you.

I have the opportunity to be in the media a lot. I am amazed at how people act when a television camera is pointed in their direction. People are much more careful, myself included, of how they act. I try not to cough or say things that might be misconstrued by those who are watching me. Cameras change people's behaviors.

TIPS FOR PATIENCE

Don't ever forget that God is watching over you. Right now as you are reading these pages, God and His witnesses, the angels, are watching you. They, along with the people in your life, are your audience. You are the host of your own reality show, called the *You Show*. How many "tapes" of your daily actions do you want to be available at heaven's Blockbuster! In case you're feeling the need to work on yourself in the presence of these heavenly beings, I've provided some tips that are sure to make your audience smile.

Prayer

The first tip I want to share with you is prayer, but don't just pray for patience. I am sure you have heard the preacher's story about the guy who prayed for patience, and in one day he lost his job, his house burned down, and he had a flat tire. Of course, that's a myth, but many of us have a concern about praying for this fruit.

If you are not intentionally trying to grow fruit, the process may be more painful than it needs to be. However, if you desire to grow spiritual fruit, I have a safe prayer for patience that you can pray. Read this and see what you think.

Lord, I ask you to help me to respond patiently to my spouse today.

This prayer can help if done on a daily basis. You can add:

I want to express Your patient love toward my spouse today. God, I know that my spouse is Your child. You were beaten and died for any sin my spouse—or I—commit today. Please, God, let me express Your patience today in responding to my spouse.

A focused intentional prayer can keep you mindful of the fruit of your agreement so that your spouse can taste from you today. Imagine how you would feel if your spouse was praying this prayer for himself or herself today. Imagine if two spouses were praying this prayer within the same marriage. Imagine if they followed through on a regular basis to respond patiently.

Imagine what this would do for your children. They would actually see both parents being patient toward one another. Imagine the influence this would have on your children's faith and character. I know we are only dreaming, but dreams often come true for those who pray and work toward being the answer to their own prayers.

Detachment

The second tip that can move you toward patience comes through detachment. So many marriage partners fall into bizarre belief patterns. Some believe their spouse is deliberately trying to be offensive or purposely causing them pain. Oh, I know every once in a while many of us get into a mood where we deliberately try to frustrate or anger our spouse by doing something due to our lack of patience. But by and large your spouse is not trying to get you going. It's important that you avoid believing that every annoying thing your spouse does is being done to annoy you. It's not all about you. Very likely your spouse would have this annoying behavior even if he or she was not married to you. Your spouse is just being his or her own human, sin-fallen self.

Detachment allows you take a step back and diffuse the situation. You may even need to step back and say aloud: "This is not about me. This is just who he/she is. He/she is not trying to be mean or spiteful, he/she is just being him[her]self." If you can step back, you will be able to react more patiently to the behavior.

The way you think personally about your spouse's behavior will dictate how you will respond. If you see the behavior as a personal attack, believing your spouse is "out to get you," your response will most likely be less patient. But if you can frame it as that person just being herself or himself, you may be able to be detached enough to be patient.

How you see your spouse's behavior is your choice. Your spouse does not control how you view him or her. You can control how you see the behavior as part of the blessing of having an imperfect and human spouse who loves you—not as an all-out alien attack to steal the joy out of your life.

You must refuse to view your partner's annoying quirks as deliberate offenses. This is a choice—you can choose to refuse your previous interpretation of your spouse's behavior by choosing a more gentle and patient way to respond.

"Stop"

After you apply prayer and detachment, a third tip I would offer in the area of patience is to "stop." That is, stop believing and behaving as if you have the power to change your spouse. God has never commanded you to change your spouse. He has only called you to love your spouse. Nowhere in Scripture do you see it spelled out, "Go thou and change thy spouse."

God alone can change a person. We are limited to the power of changing *ourselves*. Beyond changing yourself, you are powerless. You are, and are forever, powerless to change any human being including your spouse.

At first, powerlessness seems difficult. But when you truly accept your own powerlessness toward your spouse, you are finally living in reality. Once you are in reality, you will be less angry and controlling. In fact, you may actually come across as being more patient. What you are doing is accepting reality. The reality is that you cannot change your spouse.

I encourage you to *stop* doing what God has already made

impossible to do. You might as well put five hundred pounds of weight on a bar and try to bench press it! You see, if you *believe* you are supposed to be able to bench-press five hundred pounds, you will actually try to do it. After you have failed, you will try again and again. Eventually you will get mad at the five hundred pounds for being five hundred pounds. You will yell, scream, give it the dirty look, and anything else that you think will work to get the weight to cooperate with your faulty reality. You'll come up with all kinds of ideas to bench-press the five hundred pounds. You'll try to get stronger, maybe get others to help you manipulate the five hundred pounds, take steroids, try different configurations of how the weights are placed on the bench. All these out-of-control behaviors happen because you are simply believing a lie. The lie is that you are supposed to be able to bench-press five hundred pounds.

Now this may sound silly, but take a moment to put the book down and think of the silly ways you have tried to change your spouse. Start from the first year of marriage all the way up to this past month. I'll bet there is a column of failed efforts at changing your spouse, all because you believe a lie.

Where did the lie that you can change your spouse come from? God didn't give you the lie. You got this lie straight from the enemy. Just as God is trying to grow the fruit of His Spirit in your life, so too the devil attempts to grow the fruit of strife, contention, and discord in your life. Don't give entry to the devil's seeds in your life. A seed can only produce what it is. Apples produce apples, and lies produce strife.

I found out that when I was able to give up the lie that I could change Lisa, I was able to relax. After I relaxed, I found that I was much more accepting of who she is right now. I didn't need her to be better in order to love her more. I actually started to love—and like—her more, and patience seemed to be much easier for me.

How does change occur? Change occurs as a reaction or action toward your circumstances. So your changing can influence change.

There is another way change can occur. It's a powerful secret I learned on the road of marriage. To utilize this secret you must be fairly squeaky clean in your behavior toward your spouse. If you are not squeaky clean, this secret may backfire on you, so be careful.

Begin by asking yourself honestly about how your attitudes, behaviors, and service toward your spouse are currently. If you feel good about your attitudes, behaviors, and service to your spouse, proceed. Proceed to the One who designed, created, gave birth to, fed, and clothed your spouse all these years—his or her Father, the living God of all the heavens and earth.

Acknowledge who He is, and I recommend gratitude toward Him for who your spouse is. Then approach Him with gentleness, and tell Him about the situation or difficulty you are having with His child—your spouse. He alone has the power to change both you and your spouse.

Then do the dangerous part. Ask if the problem is *you*.

Father and Father-in-law God, if I am believing wrongly, acting wrongly, or in any way the problem, correct me.

Change me, and don't let me be wicked in any way to Your precious child—my spouse.

Then be quiet, and see if the God of heaven and earth has anything to say to you. If He does, thank Him for the correction. Repent and follow His direction to you immediately.

If He does not speak to you with correction and your own heart does not convict you of any sin, proceed gently:

Father, if I am not the issue, then change in my spouse what You alone can see so we can both glorify You.

Now be silent; don't give God advice or any insight about your spouse. Leave your prayer place with faith that God is able and willing to change your spouse. Change may not be immediate, but I have experienced miracles of God where He changed me or Lisa. I remember a couple of gridlocks Lisa and I were in that left me feeling frustrated. God did something to effect a change in Lisa, and the change was nothing short of miraculous.

Turn yourself and your spouse over to God; He is able and willing to make change. *Patience avoids trying to change the behavior in your spouse that you struggle with.*

The power of patience

A fourth tip to increase patience toward your spouse is to experience the pure power of patience. In Proverbs 16:32 we read that a patient man wins over a city. Think back to the biblical period of time when the Proverbs were written. What was the primary protective structure of a city in Old Testament times? It was the big thick wall that surrounded the city.

I can't think of a better picture of an angry person than of a walled-off city. How would a patient man win such a city? Why does the Bible tell us it was a "patient man," not a cruel man, a strong man, a clever man, or a great warrior?

I have thought a lot about this proverb. I remember stories and movies about wars where a general would camp outside of a city. He would command his troops to encircle the city so no one could leave. He would cut off its water and food supplies and wait. He would wait while the people in the enemy city became weak, dehydrated, and starved. Soon they would begin to fight internally, and eventually they opened their gates to their well-fed and watered conqueror. In many of these stories, patience was the force the general used. Patience is raw power.

Anger needs a food source. Your impatience is the food source of anger. As you react, overreact, or just act plain silly, anger becomes stronger. It mocks your impatience, turns the focus inward toward you, and makes the situation impossible to deal with.

However, I have discovered that anger cannot be fed or nourished by patience. Patience is to anger what kryptonite is to Superman. With the kryptonite of patience, you will not look foolish. You won't use a faulty rationale to try to change the circumstances. You will be together, confident, and calm in the way you respond to your spouse. With patience, your spouse will soon be willing to open up and get honest about the situation.

This doesn't happen the first time you are patient. But like the general who waits day after day, as you counter your spouse's anger and frustration with your own patience, soon the enemy's fruit of discord and division can no longer feed the attitudes and feelings of your spouse.

The power of patience is that of an intentional force. Patience works with the precision of an intentional blow from a black belt expert. Patience is an action. Patience is not some passive state of agreement or being walked all over.

My wife is pretty close to being a saint and rarely gets angry unless I, or someone else, have created a very difficult situation for her. But one day Lisa was what I call *fussy.* I could tell I could easily tip her in the wrong direction if I wanted to. So I did what any Christian man would do in my condition. I prayed, "God, please give me wisdom." As she walked down the steps in the garage to enter my car, she opened the door and sat in her comfortable seat. As she placed her drink in the cup holder, the Holy Spirit gave me these words to say to her: "Lisa, I am more committed to loving you and enjoying you all day than you are to any mood. I will love you more at the end of the day than I do now."

It was as if I drop-kicked that fussy mood right outside my car. She looked at me with those ever-green eyes, and smiled, and, yes, we had a great day. The Lord showed me how to purposely, with intent, harness the raw power of nature.

Let me give you another example of the power of patience. As I shared earlier, in the early stages of our relationship, we read all the marriage books we could read. Somehow, and honestly, I don't know how, the question of infidelity came up—that is, my possible infidelity. I asked Lisa what she would do if I ever was unfaithful.

She looked me straight in the eye, and with all her powerful soul she said, "I will love you, forgive you, and stay with you." She communicated such a powerful sense of patience it was like a power missile shot through my soul, taking with it any desire to ever hurt someone who would love me that patiently.

Patience is power. When I am patient with myself, Lisa, my children, or any of my staff or counselors, it is always a better experience than if I responded impatiently.

The seed of patience

Patience is a seed. Galatians 5:22 lists patience as one of the fruit of the Spirit. All fruits have seeds. All fruit trees grow in the same way: the fruit ripens, falls off the tree, and the rotten fruit gives way to seeds. The seeds go into the ground and, with the conditions of soil, rain, and light, create a new fruit tree. This process has been going on for thousands of years.

The power of a seed is incredible. Remember that humans are still just fancy dirt; like Adam, we were all created from dirt. When we perform an act of patience such as a listening ear, silence about a spouse's mistake, or a laugh instead of a glare, we are sowing patience into our spouse's being. *Patience allows us to discipline our responses to respond positively to the difficult behavior we are dealing with from our spouse.* Our response becomes a powerful seed.

Seeds like these don't grow instantly. Seeds take time to mature. As you intentionally plant the seeds of patience, you will not reap an instant response, but you will reap eventually. And, as you become more patient, you will receive more patience in return.

The sin nature will remain inside us until death. There is absolutely no doubt that there will be times when you will sin in your behavior toward your spouse and will need his or her patience. And there will never be a time when your spouse will not need your patience. Keep planting the seed of patience in the soil of your spouse's life, because there will be days when you need to eat the fruit of patience that has been grown.

Remember the times when your spouse sows patience into your soul. In this way the principle of sowing and reaping can happen in your marriage relationship. Sow like the wind, and reap a harvest when the season comes for you to need a harvest.

Forbearance

Forbearance, my last tip for you, may not seem like a pleasant one, but it does help when your goal is to be more patient. Forbearance means that there are just some things in life that will not change in a lifetime—or at least not your lifetime.

You will simply need to forbear the things about your spouse that are unchanging. It may not seem to be very glamorous or rewarding, but in your goal to become more Christlike, you must remember that it will take a measure of forbearance.

Being patient can motivate you to change, making you more compatible with your spouse as you modify your own behaviors that can be annoying. Patience can help you through this season with your spouse.

You and your spouse may feel that you need to communicate to each other the little things that bother you about each other, but this doesn't always bring about change. Just think about how many times the Holy Spirit has reminded you about change. If you take a moment, you will discover that there are some things He has been talking about with you for years.

The Holy Spirit has exercised forbearance about many of your less than wonderful characteristics. Forbearing your spouse's shortcomings is an opportunity for you to grow the fruit of patience.

Don't express your forbearance grudgingly. *A good sense of humor is important when you are practicing forbearance.* I have found that if I can laugh, I can enjoy my spouse instead of merely tolerating her. She is the daughter of God, and she has flaws. Her flaws can be cute or annoying, depending on where my heart is. So see if you can smile before you start talking to yourself about the wonderful gift of your spouse.

My Commitment to Patience

All right, we have talked much about patience. It's time to make our love agreement to help improve our marriages.

I WILL NOT TRY TO CHANGE THINGS ABOUT MY SPOUSE THAT I DO NOT LIKE BUT WILL MODIFY MY BEHAVIORS THAT ANNOY MY PARTNER.

Before we make our agreement, let's first officially break our old agreements with behaviors and attitudes of impatience. Let us pray:

Lord Jesus, I confess as sin all my thoughts, attitudes, beliefs, and behaviors of impatience toward my spouse. I break any agreements I have had with impatient thoughts, attitudes, beliefs, or behaviors. Thank You for breaking my prior agreements with impatience, in Your name.

Now, let's make our love agreement of patience. Let us pray:

In the name of Jesus, I officially make an agreement to be patient with my spouse. I fully accept that both my spouse and I are completely imperfect, yet loved by You. I command my mind, will, and emotions to create new thoughts, beliefs, attitudes, and behaviors that are patient. I commit myself to the love agreement to be patient with my spouse throughout my marriage. Jesus, I pray for Your power through the Holy Spirit to assist me to be patient, in Jesus' name.

That's terrific! You have made a love agreement toward being patient. You and I know it's a journey—actually, a lifelong journey. In making this love agreement, you have put your feet on the path of patience. By making a love agreement, you command the rudder of your heart to head in the direction of patience. Now, to make your journey more likely to be successful, let's talk about practical goals you might have to face in the journey of becoming more patient with your spouse.

GOALS FOR PATIENCE

Underline each of the following goals you are willing to make a commitment to keep, and for each goal you underline, fill in the specific behavior you will use to reach that goal.

1. For the next sixty days, I will pray daily for God to help me respond patiently to my spouse.

   _____

2. I will identify one area where I am usually impatient and will record my responses on a daily basis.

   _____

3. I will make a list of five things about my spouse that cause me to become impatient. I will write a one-page paper telling how I am guilty of the same behavior.

_____

4. I will practice not allowing myself to think that my spouse's behavior is about me. I refuse to believe his or her motive is to cause harm to me.

_____

5. For one month, I will change a behavioral response to see if change occurs.

_____

6. I will do a word study on the word *patience* in the Bible.

_____

7. I will smile when my spouse does something that typically causes me to be impatient.

_____

8. I will behave as if this is the very first time my spouse is in need of my patience in this area.

_____

LAST STEP

As in any love agreement, making the agreement to be patient is just the beginning. To be ultimately successful, after choosing a goal you must take action to move one step further.

You can make that move by selecting one of your goals and measuring your success at reaching the goal. It is crucial that you measure your progress to really evaluate how successful you are in your love agreement.

So with your goal in mind, create some form of measurement. Place this measurement on a piece of paper that you will see regularly. You may choose to tape it to your mirror, place it on the night table beside your bed, or even carry it in the back of your Bible. Record your progress daily. Over time you will be amazed to see the change in the way you behave, and even change in the way you feel and think about your spouse. There is real power in a love agreement actively measured over time.

The principle of accountability will help here. Check in at least weekly with a friend you trust, or even someone else who is doing the love agreements—that makes it even more fun. Go over your goals and progress with your accountability partner of the same gender.

If your accountability partner is agreeable, pray about each other's goals to improve your marriages. The level of friendship you have with your accountability partner as you pray, laugh, and encourage each other through this season of your love agreements will help improve your marriage.

You are the power of one. You are armed with all the power of Christ through the Holy Spirit. You can slay impatience and plant and harvest the fruit of patience. You are allowed to be a vineyard of patience for your lover, best friend, and child of God—your spouse.

Patience is powerful. Remember that you already have this seed of God inside of you. So let it out, measure it, and have lots of fun as you become more patient.

$\mathcal{L}$OVE $\mathcal{A}$GREEMENT #3

When I have offended my spouse, I will

quickly ask for forgiveness. And I will

forgive my spouse's offenses in my heart

even before being asked.

Chapter Five

Love Agreement #3:
FORGIVENESS

om and Renee were a great Christian couple. To know them was to love them. They were successful in business, had great children in a Christian school, and were both involved in ministries in the megachurch they have attended for nearly twenty years.

So what was a couple like them doing in a counseling office? They didn't know the answer to that question when they walked through the door; they just felt like something was missing in their relationship. They couldn't really pinpoint the problem to any large sin in their life. There was no infidelity. They had healthy attitudes about finances, sex, and friends.

Yet something was blocking the depth of intimacy they had experienced earlier in their marriage. After some information gathering and observation, together we determined that the culprit was *unforgiveness*. They discovered that a lot of little sins had begun to clog up the love they once experienced.

Karla Donaldson's story is quite different than Tom and Renee's. Karla was a thirty-two-year-old Christian woman and had been married for nine years to her husband. She had two small children, one of whom she was homeschooling. She had a master's degree in education and worked part time as a dance instructor.

She thought her world was perfect. She had a husband who loved her and belonged to a cell group that she and her family attended. She was faithful in her Bible studies and, overall, was a very warm, gracious type of woman.

Then out of the blue she received a phone call from the police in a city about fifty miles from where they lived. They asked her if she was Mrs. Donaldson. With a pounding heart and sweating hands, she said *yes*. Awful thoughts poured through her mind that someone she loved might have been hurt in an accident.

But that wasn't the message she received. Officer Timmons asked her if she would mind coming to pick up her husband.

"My husband?" she asked.

Officer Timmons said, "Yes."

"Why, what's going on? This must be a mistake," she frantically replied with a crackling in her voice and tears running down her face, overwhelmed and perplexed.

"Ma'am," Officer Timmons said in a calm but secure voice, "are you sitting down?"

"Not yet," she answered.

"I recommend you sit down and let me tell you what happened today. Your husband was caught in a sting operation today with thirty-six other men who were soliciting prostitutes. I know you're probably in shock if this is the first time you are hearing this. He was tape-recorded asking for sexual services and gave sixty dollars to a female officer posing as a prostitute."

Karla describes this as the worst day of her life. She can still articulate what she was wearing on the way to pick her husband up from jail. In Karla's case, she knew exactly why she was in counseling.

She found out from her husband, Daryl, that this wasn't a one-time thing. He felt addicted to self-behavior, pornography, the Internet, and prostitutes. These were no little sins for our Christian wife. She had been hurt and betrayed deeply. Although after this incident Daryl sought help and went to support groups, things remained difficult in their marriage. Nine months into his recovery, Daryl actually took a polygraph exam to prove to Karla beyond a shadow of doubt that he was free from all his sexually addictive behaviors and immorality.

Karla believed Daryl, but she said, "I just feel stuck on moving forward. It's like I am blocked from really giving him my heart again."

Karla was running into a very normal problem, one that any woman who is brave enough to continue her marriage after infidelity would face. That normal problem was forgiveness.

Myths About Forgiveness

Forgiveness will need to paint a wide swath in your marriage relationship. We will discuss forgiveness from several different angles in order to really help you experience the full power of your love agreement on forgiveness. But first, let's expose a few myths about forgiveness.

I must confront the person in order to offer that person my forgiveness.

The first myth about forgiveness is that the person who has sinned against you has to be present in order for you to forgive him or her. Some people don't believe they can forgive someone unless they are right in front of them. For me personally, most of the many people I have forgiven in my life were not present when I forgave them, and yet I was able to forgive them anyway.

I have seen vast numbers of my clients forgive those who hurt them without the perpetrators of that hurt being present. Some clients have been able to forgive many types of abuse and abandonment from those who were supposed to love them—including the spouses.

Forgiveness is possible whether the person is present or not. Since forgiveness is a decision, this decision can be made without the person being present. It is similar to the example of a president or governor making the decision to pardon a prisoner, regardless of the crime, even though that person is sitting in a jail cell somewhere far away from the official giving the pardon.

The prisoner isn't taken to the president's or governor's office and then pardoned—not at all. The prisoner stays in his or her cell and may be totally unaware that a pardon is about to be given. Most likely, it will be after the pardon has been granted that the prisoner will be notified about it. The pardon takes place without the prisoner's presence.

In this chapter I will suggest some exercises for you to use to give forgiveness. As you use them, remember that the forgiveness you offer will be just as complete in your heart whether or not the person you are forgiving is present.

That person is going to have to repent first.

You may believe that before you can forgive someone, that person must repent for his or her actions against you. This is not true at all. It is great if that person repents, but it's not necessary for your spouse, or anyone else for that matter, to repent in order for you to offer your forgiveness.

Forgiveness is your decision alone. If you believe that a person who wronged you must first repent before you offer forgiveness, in essence you have given the power of forgiveness over to that person. That person is making the choice for you of when you will be allowed to exercise forgiveness and find freedom from the impact of his or her sin in your life. Obviously, the power of when you forgive should not be given away—it is a choice that you make, and you choose the time when you should do it.

Remember this: Christ died for us while we were yet sinners. (See Romans 5:8.) He didn't wait for humanity to ask forgiveness before He sacrificed Himself for the forgiveness of our sins. No, He exercised His right and power to forgive you even though you were not present or able to ask for forgiveness two thousand years ago.

You also can exercise your right and power to forgive your spouse without your spouse repenting. Hallelujah, that's great news, because it means you can free yourself from the impact of that wrong by offering forgiveness at will.

Forgiveness is not just something that you have the right to give to another person. As a Christian, Christ has commanded you to forgive. (See Matthew 6:12–15.) The power to forgive and the command to forgive have been given to you by God. You control this power, and you have control of when and where you offer forgiveness, regardless of whether the other person has repented or not.

I have to see change in that person before I can forgive.

It is a myth to believe that a person must change before you can forgive him or her. I can't tell you how many times I have heard Christian men and women say this. I firmly believe that change is possible—and necessary—for everyone. That is the only way we can become more Christlike. However, not all spouses will change. Even if you are the greatest, most loving spouse God ever created, it doesn't mean your spouse is going to choose to change.

Whether or not your spouse changes is not a prerequisite for you to forgive or not forgive. Let's just get real about this for a minute. Sometimes demanding that your spouse change before you forgive him or her for some wrong is nothing more than an excuse, or worse, self-righteous, moral superiority! Such an attitude just causes you to wall yourself off from your spouse or others.

Jesus didn't say to me, "Doug, you change; then I will forgive you." If He did that, I would be on an endless process of trying to be good enough to be forgiven. No, what Jesus said was, "Doug, I forgive you." He even knew that I would sin again. He even knew I would sin *in the same area* again. He even knew it would take years, even decades, before I would gain victory over those sins.

What was God thinking to forgive a sinner like me before I changed? I think He was thinking that His forgiveness would eventually penetrate my heart and that my will to sin would surface less and less as the likeness of Christ grew more and more predominant in me. His approach to forgiveness is so much better than waiting for my spouse to change.

All that I need is a gentle reminder by the Holy Spirit about how much sin Christ has forgiven me of to be more forgiving of my precious but slightly flawed Lisa. You see, forgiveness can flow from you to your spouse by your choice, whether your spouse is present or not. What a great force forgiveness can be in your life and in your marriage.

The love agreement of forgiveness is up to you to effect in your life. You don't even need your spouse's involvement or confession of sin. Forgiveness is the gift you give—just as Christ has given it to you.

HONESTY

As Christians we are sinners saved by the grace of God. The only requirement we had to meet was a willingness to confess our sins and ask God to take over our lives. Yet as I travel around the country speaking at marriage conferences and in churches, I can't begin to count the many men and women who have shared with me the fact that their spouses never apologize or ask for forgiveness.

As a counselor this is so hard for me to comprehend. You see, I realize that there is no marriage anywhere where sin never surfaces. Even in a good marriage with two mature Christians, there are going to be times when both marriage partners sin in their actions toward the other spouse. This will happen often, at least weekly, and in some homes, it may happen nearly every day. So for a marriage partner to be unable to *own up* to his or her sin readily tells me that person is truly in denial. Denial in these things creates terrible tension for the other spouse and for the marriage relationship.

Some couples like to play the game "Your sin is bigger than mine" or "Only your sin counts." Those games solve nothing and merely create marriage problems. In this chapter I want to help you get a practical handle on sin.

In 1 Corinthians 13:4–8 we read:

> Love is patient, love is kind. It does not envy, it does not boast, it is not proud. It is not rude; it is not self-seeking; it is not easily angered; it keeps no record of wrongs. Love does not delight in evil but rejoices with the truth. It always protects, always trusts, always hopes, always perseveres. Love never fails.

Wow, this scripture is convicting. If I am impatient, rude, or selfish, I am actually sinning. Therefore, it is very important that you learn to be very honest about your sins. You may be tempted to use this list on your spouse to measure how he or she is failing. However, although that might be tempting, it won't help change yourself or your marriage.

I have been helping you to understand that the love agreements in this book are something one person does that impacts the marriage. You see, the more honest you are about your sins in your marriage, the more potential there is for your honesty to change things in your marriage relationship. *As you develop a ritual of asking for forgiveness of your sins, like, "Honey, I sinned again by getting angry," or "Honey, I need you to forgive me for not being patient," you begin to set up a new paradigm in your marriage.* The paradigm is, *"I sin,"* and, *"I need to acknowledge and own my sin."*

It may take time for this new way of believing, behaving, and communicating to work its way into the fabric of your marriage. But once your spouse sees that you can be honest, this gives them a greater opportunity to be honest with you. For some of you it may take weeks or months for you to believe that you sin and need to be forgiven, but continue to be consistent at it.

ANGER

Anger can be a very important issue to address before we look at the forgiveness exercises. Many people harbor anger toward their spouse. Are you one of these people?

As a counselor, I know that anger will have to be addressed first before you can truly forgive. So many Christians go to counselors with problems of abuse, trauma, and other kinds of wounding from others. Many times they are told to forgive but are given no instructions about how to heal the wound. Years after the wounding occurred, often they wonder why they still feel wounded or act wounded even though they forgave the person who caused the wounding.

When we experience significant trauma from our spouse or others we become wounded. These wounds are three-dimensional: spirit, soul, and body. It will take a spirit, soul, and body solution to eradicate the wounds. Remember the example of Karla I used earlier? She became emotionally stuck because of her unrealized, legitimate anger. Once she was able to do the Cleanse the Temple exercise she was able to move more quickly through to forgiveness in a genuine manner.

The Cleanse the Temple exercise is something you can do without your spouse being aware of the pent-up anger you harbor toward him or her. As a part of this exercise you will be writing a letter. However, you will never, ever show this letter to your spouse. That would not be helpful.

You can learn to deal with the anger you have toward your spouse alone. Just as we discussed about forgiveness, they don't have to be there, confess, or change; and you can deal with this alone. Once you have actually done the Cleanse the Temple exercise, your spirit, soul, and body will be able to do the exercises you have ahead of you on forgiveness.

Cleanse the Temple

In my earlier book *Intimacy: A 100-Day Guide to Lasting Relationships*, I introduced the Cleanse the Temple exercise to help couples overcome the hurt that happens at times in marriage.[1] I think this is a very effective exercise that you can use to remove a lot of the pain that you may carry in your soul. This pain may be from family of origin issues caused by neglect, abuse, or abandonment. The pain you carry may be from childhood sexual abuse or rape. Some pain carried in your soul is from your spouse. In some Christian marriages, spouses traumatize one another or deprive one another to such a degree that the anger appears overwhelming.

Anger can build up in your soul until the size of your wounds makes it difficult to be intimate. Even though you did not cause the wounds, you are now responsible to heal from them. Similar to walking outside and getting shot by a sniper, you are 100 percent responsible to heal from the wound, even though your spouse is 100 percent responsible for causing the wound.

This is a very important concept to understand, because in our culture victim status is power. This power is manipulated to make other people pay or is used to keep from accepting full responsibility for yourself or the direction of your life.

I can attest, as much as anyone else, to the fact that life can be painful. Some people enjoy creating pain for others. I was conceived in adultery. My conception caused a divorce in my mother's first marriage. She then married my legal father, thus my name is *Weiss*.

He was an alcoholic, and my mother and he divorced after having three girls of their own. My three half-sisters and I were placed into separate foster homes and moved from home to home for the next few years. Eventually my mom took us back out of the foster homes. At the age of fifteen, I was sexually abused. There are more things that I could tell you about my life, but I think you can understand that my soul has seen some days of pain.

But the day came when I realized that even though I didn't cause the mess my life was in, I was 100 percent responsible for cleaning up the mess. God assured me that He would be with me in this process, but I had to be obedient and not allow the pain from the past to justify why I was not becoming all that I could be. For those of you who need to heal from similar issues, what I am about to ask you to do is going to be difficult work.

I sincerely don't believe that I would be as intimate and open with my wife, Lisa, today if I had not cleaned up the anger I felt about my past during the early years of our marriage. So I encourage you that if you have wounds others have inflicted on your life, continue to read and to follow through with the homework assigned.

The Cleanse the Temple exercise has its roots in the biblical example of Jesus cleansing the temple. An account of this event is found in each Gospel. Take a moment to study this biblical example.

> When it was almost time for the Jewish Passover, Jesus went up to Jerusalem. In the temple courts he found men selling cattle, sheep and doves, and others sitting at tables exchanging money. So he

made a whip out of cords, and drove all from the temple area, both sheep and cattle; he scattered the coins of the money changers and overturned their tables. To those who sold doves he said "Get these out of here! How dare you turn my Father's house into a market!"

His disciples remembered that it is written: "Zeal for your house will consume me." Then the Jews demanded of him, "What miraculous sign can you show us to prove your authority to do all this?" Jesus answered them, "Destroy this temple, and I will raise it again in three days." The Jews replied, "It has taken forty-six years to build this temple, and you are going to raise it in three days?" But the temple he had spoken of was his body. After he was raised from the dead, his disciples recalled what he had said. Then they believed the Scripture and the words that Jesus had spoken.

—JOHN 2:13–22

Within this biblical account of Jesus cleansing the temple, we find the principles for our Cleanse the Temple exercise. We will review the four major principles, and then we will walk through the practical application of each principle.

BIBLICAL PRINCIPLES

Principle 1—the temple

In this account of Jesus cleansing the temple, "temple" refers to the physical temple in Jerusalem. The Jews asked Jesus: "What miraculous sign can you show us to prove your authority to do all this?" (v. 18).

Jesus responded to them by saying, "'Destroy this temple, and I will raise it again in three days.' The Jews replied, 'It has taken forty-six years to build this temple, and you are going to raise it in three days?' But the temple he had spoken of was His body" (vv. 19–21). This is the first insight we have that Jesus was changing the dwelling place of God from the physical temple to the temple of a human being.

Paul developed this thought later when he recorded that we, as Christian believers, are the temples of God.

> Don't you know that you yourselves are God's temple and that God's Spirit lives in you? If anyone destroys God's temple, God will destroy him; for God's temple is sacred, and you are that temple.
>
> —1 CORINTHIANS 3:16–17

It has always been God's plan to dwell inside of us. We are His holy temples. Our temples can get defiled through many avenues, including manipulations, abuses, and neglect from others. When we get defiled by life, our temples get defiled and need to be cleansed.

It is interesting to note in this passage that Jesus, the owner of the temple, was the one who took full responsibility for cleaning His temple. The moneychangers and sellers of doves were the ones who had made the mess in the temple in Jerusalem, and He could have made them clean up their own mess. But He didn't. He cleansed the temple.

We are the possessors of our temples. If your temple gets defiled through the abuse of others, you are the one that needs to clean it up. You are actually the *only one* who can clean your temple.

Even if your spouse caused the defilement, he or she cannot clean it out of your temple. Your spouse can say, "I'm sorry," but that doesn't get rid of the muck or defilement that has already been placed inside your soul. You need to clean that mess up. The fact that Jesus took responsibility for cleaning His own temple gives us the clear message that we can clean our own temples as well.

Principle 2—He identified the sin.

Jesus stated, "Get these out of here! How dare you turn my Father's house into a market!" (John 2:16). In Luke 19:46, Mark 11:17, and Matthew 21:13, the rendering of Jesus' words are slightly stronger: "'It is written,' he said to them, 'My house will be called a house of prayer'; but you have made it 'a den of robbers'" (Luke 19:46).

Jesus was letting them know what their offense was, what it was that required Him to cleanse the temple. They had taken something holy and had misused it in order to profit for themselves. You can apply this concept to your own hurt. Most of the people who have hurt you had no concept of your holiness or preciousness. Yet you felt used or abused during the incidents when you were wounded. In one of the exercises of Cleanse the Temple, you will need to be able to identify the sin or damage that has been done to you by those who have defiled your temple.

Principle 3—He engaged His anger.

Jesus was able to engage the anger at the injustice both physically and verbally. His turning over the table was probably quite a scene. I am sure that is why the Jews asked Him about His authority to create such a ruckus.

This wasn't an example of Jesus just having a bad day. This was an act of His will. This was a thought-through act of obedience. This is an important point to understand, because an act of your will is required to clean your temple. Once you walk through the rest of the exercises, I believe that it will be an act of obedience as well.

Some have asked me how I know this was something Jesus premeditated. John's account of the cleansing of the temple states this: "He found men selling cattle, sheep and doves, and others sitting at tables exchanging money. So he made a whip out of cords" (John 2:14–15). In these verses you get the feeling that Jesus was looking around and witnessing the people's mistreatment of His holy temple. Then He took the time to make a whip out of a bunch of cords. I don't know how long it took Jesus to make a whip, maybe minutes or hours, but it shows me that He had intention on using that whip and committed some premeditated time before He went in to cleanse His temple.

Like Jesus in this example, you will also be making choices to prioritize your time to prepare for cleansing your temple. Be encouraged that others who have taken the time to prioritize and prepare to clean their temples have received great breakthroughs in their lives.

Principle 4—The temple was restored to its original order.

The example of Jesus cleansing the temple offers a picture of how to heal your wounds inside your temple. After He engaged His righteous rage, His temple was cleansed. He took full responsibility to cleanse His temple and to restore it to its original order. So, too, you alone will be able to cleanse your temple from its wounds and restore it to its original order.

PRACTICAL APPLICATION

During the years of my work with couples and individuals in both inpatient psychiatric hospitals and in outpatient settings, I have seen many wounded souls. These wounds are harbored deep inside at the core of their being. Many of these souls had experienced trauma in one form or another.

When you experience trauma, you experience it in all three levels of your being—spirit, soul, and body. All three parts of your being have been defiled, injured, or neglected.

When I train therapists across this country, I stress that trauma survivors have been affected in spirit, soul, and body. Then I ask them, "Why do we think, then, that we can just treat trauma cognitively and expect people to heal? If the trauma affects all three dimensions of a person, doesn't it make sense that the healing of trauma involves all three aspects of the spirit, soul, and body?"

I tell you this, you may have people who have hurt you significantly. You may have presumed that you have forgiven them, however, you still have the bullet deep inside. If so, it doesn't necessarily mean that you have not forgiven them. Perhaps you just haven't cleansed your temple yet.

This concept may seem foreign or uncomfortable to you at first. So let me assure you of the importance of this experience by telling you that my experience with people who have agreed to cleanse the temple has been nothing short of miraculous. I have seen sexual abuse survivors heal very quickly after this exercise. I have seen women who were sexually betrayed by their Christian husbands suddenly be able to move through the stages of grief and forgiveness so much more quickly than those who refuse to cleanse their temple.

I encourage you to keep an open mind and try this exercise if you feel your spouse or others have injured you. After (not before) you do this exercise, you will be able to tell if it has been effective or not.

THE CLEANSE THE TEMPLE EXERCISE

1. Write an anger letter.

Begin your exercise by writing an anger letter to someone who has hurt you. But remember, you are never going to send this letter! I often tell my clients to imagine this person is in the room and unable to talk or move. You can say whatever you need to say to him or her in this letter. Don't suppress your feelings. Let out all the thoughts and feelings of hate, disgust, and anguish that have been robbing your soul of life. This letter is not an "I forgive you" letter. That comes later. This is the place where you rid yourself of the anger that has been a part of your soul. These wounds make intimacy more difficult for someone in marriage. Someone who is wounded acts a lot differently in a marriage than someone who is healed. I know from experience. This first step is simply to express your anger in letter form toward the person who caused you pain.

2. Be prepared to warm up.

In Jesus' situation, He made a whip for Himself. I don't recommend whips, but a padded baseball bat or racket could be helpful. First, warm up your body. Take your bat, and hit your mattress or pillow, first with small hits, then medium, large, and extra large hits. I recommend you do this three consecutive times. Then warm up your voice as well. Using the word *no* along with the hits, do small, medium, large, and extra large nos with your voice while hitting. This may feel awkward, but removing this buildup of pain from your soul and spirit feels wonderfully liberating, which is why you want to be physically warmed up.

It is probably a good idea to make sure you are home alone when you are warming up. I would suggest also that you disconnect the phone to avoid being disturbed.

(Note: If you have a heart condition or another medical condition, talk to your doctor before taking part in this exercise.)

3. Read the letter aloud.

After your physical warm-up, read the letter you wrote aloud. If your offender's name is "Toby," then you would read the letter aloud like this: "Toby, how could you have done this to me? I trusted you!..."

Of course, Toby is not in the room listening to you read the letter. The exercise of reading aloud is for your benefit and healing, not to confront the person who has wronged you.

4. *Engage the anger physically and verbally.*

After reading your letter, put it down and pick up your bat. Once again you can hit the bed or pillow and let "Toby" symbolically have it. You can yell, scream, cry ... but let the infection out that has been robbing you. You can symbolically tell him, "Your secrets are no longer controlling me." "You are to blame for my anger!" You have no limits as to what you can say to your offender. For once, let go of all the control that is keeping this wound infected. Let it out!

This can last anywhere from fifteen minutes to an hour. Usually your body will let you know when you are done—spiritually, emotionally, and physically—and ready to put the offense, and your anger, behind you.

It is worth the effort you are taking to get the hurt and anger out. Someone has given you something toxic. You have been unhealthy ever since, but after it is removed from you, you will feel so much better.[2]

COMMENTS

When you do your Cleanse the Temple exercise, you should only work on one offender at a time. If you have been offended by three different people, then you should be ready for three different Cleanse the Temple sessions. *Do not* try to complete this exercise just once, covering all the different people who have offended you. Each "bullet" needs to be taken out separately.

If several people have caused you trauma prior to or during your marriage, make a list of them. Start with the least painful trauma and work your way up to the larger offenses. This way, you get better skilled at the exercise and will know what to expect.

The experiences with the Cleanse the Temple exercise for each person may give you different insights for the future. Sometimes it is the smallest offense that has been causing you the greatest anger. It is so important to deal with each offender because until you do, you will continue to carry the pain inside. If you do that, you will wall yourself off from the people in your life now, trying to protect yourself from being hurt and hindering you from being able to express intimacy with the ones you love now. This will only create problems for your marriage relationship today.

You may have your own thoughts about the Cleanse the Temple exercise. It may seem foolish or not appropriate for you. Before you dismiss it as not for you, think about the past pain you have experienced. Is it affecting your intimacy in your marriage relationship? Are you tired of feeling hurt and angry? Have your past attempts to "just forget about it" failed? Have you even tried to choose forgiveness and still been unable to put the pain behind you? Then why don't you try this exercise? It may be the tool that sets you free with God's help.

First Things First

First things first when it comes to forgiveness. As a counselor, I have found that if you have a problem forgiving yourself, you will also have limitations in truly forgiving your spouse on any ongoing basis.

That is because you have not accepted self-forgiveness deep within for the mistakes from the past. This lack of forgiveness of self doesn't allow you to release others through forgiveness. It's as if you are saying, "I have to pay for my sins, and so should you." Please realize that this is not done at a conscious level; however, it still is a necessary problem to address so that ultimately you can be successful in your love agreement of forgiveness.

An Exercise for Self-Forgiveness

I want to share with you a very effective exercise that I have used with clients in my counseling office for well over a decade. It is also one that I recommended in my earlier book *Intimacy: A 100-Day Guide to Lasting Relationships*.[3] Just reading about this exercise will not impact you in the area of self-forgiveness. However, doing the exercise can be a life-changing experience. Many of my clients have read about this exercise before coming to see me. But because they only read about it and did not practice it, they were unsuccessful in dealing with the unforgiveness deep within. But once they did the exercise, they were amazed at how effective it really was.

For this exercise, place two chairs facing each other. The chair on the left will be chair A for our discussion. The chair on the right will be chair B.

1. Assume the role of the offender in chair A.

Sit down in chair A to start this exercise. In chair A you are going to role-play yourself. You will imagine that you are talking to yourself in chair B. For example, in my case real Doug in chair A was talking to imagined Doug in chair B.

As the real person, I want you to own your sin. Speaking aloud, apologize to yourself, and ask forgiveness for the sins you committed toward yourself.

The conversation might go like this: "I need you to forgive me for..." The list of sins will vary from person to person. Include sexual, relational, financial, and other sins you can remember.

2. Role-play your response as the one offended.

When you are finished talking while sitting in chair A, move physically into chair B. Imagine that you have just concluded listening to all that was said to you from chair A. Now it is time for you to respond. It is very important that you be very honest with whatever you say from chair B. If you discover that you can forgive yourself for the things confessed from chair A, great.

Some people, for whatever reason, will find it a difficult process to forgive themselves. Still others will not be able to forgive themselves at all. Just be honest in the responses you make from chair B.

This exercise is not patterned to get you to actually forgive yourself but rather to assess where you are in the forgiveness process.

If you discover that you were able to forgive yourself, return to sit in chair A. But if you were unable to forgive yourself, you can stop the exercise and try again in a month to see where you are at that time. Repeat this self-forgiveness exercise monthly until you feel you have honestly forgiven yourself.

3. Role-play the offender's response to forgiveness.

If you forgave yourself, you are now back in chair A. Respond aloud to the forgiveness you received from your statements in chair B. When you have completed your response, remain sitting there for a moment and let your heart feel the forgiveness. This may be the first time you truly extended forgiveness toward yourself in any tangible way. Remember that you are truly worth the effort you have taken to extend forgiveness to yourself.

It has been my clinical experience that if a person can truly forgive himself, he is well on his way to becoming more successful in keeping the love agreement of forgiveness toward his spouse.

AN EXERCISE FOR GOD'S FORGIVENESS

Now, let's move on in the area of forgiveness. This time, sitting in chair A, you are role-playing yourself again. This time, sitting in chair B is Jesus. As before, you will own, apologize, and ask aloud for Jesus to forgive you for your sinful actions that wronged your spouse.

When you have completed asking Jesus for forgiveness, move to sit in chair B. Now respond, as you believe Jesus would respond, to your request to be forgiven.

When you have completed sharing Jesus' response to your request of forgiveness, move back to chair A. Now respond to Jesus' forgiveness of the sins you confessed. As before, after responding to Jesus' forgiveness, give yourself a minute or so to feel the forgiveness of Jesus in your heart.

For many, this may be the first time you have actually experienced the forgiveness of your sin from Jesus. For so many Christians, forgiveness is a *concept,* not an *experience.* The experience of forgiveness is a great asset for you as you move forward to keep your love agreement of forgiveness.[4]

AN EXERCISE FOR FORGIVING YOUR SPOUSE

The third exercise in the chairs will help you to extend forgiveness to your spouse. Begin by sitting in chair A. This time you will role-play your spouse and will be speaking hypothetically to yourself in chair B. As your spouse, role-play your spouse apologizing, owning, and asking forgiveness for the sins he or she committed against you. As your spouse, you would state, "I need you to forgive me for . . ." This is what your spouse would say to you if he or she was actually sitting in chair A.

When you have finished asking forgiveness, move to chair B. Now you are yourself, and you have just heard your spouse ask for forgiveness. You are ready to respond. It is so important to be honest. If you are able to forgive your spouse, great. However, if you are not able to extend forgiveness at this time, stop the exercise. You now know where you are in the forgiveness process. If you can't forgive today, do this exercise every two weeks until you can extend forgiveness.

If you were ready to forgive your spouse, do so with your response from chair B, and then go back to sit in chair A. From this chair, role-play the response of your spouse to the forgiveness you just extended. Then be still and experience that forgiveness.[5]

EXTENDING GOD'S FORGIVENESS TO YOUR SPOUSE

For this last forgiveness exercise, place yourself in chair A where you are again role-playing your spouse. Now, as your spouse, own, apologize for your sinful actions, and ask forgiveness of Jesus who is hypothetically sitting in chair B. Say, "Jesus, I need You to forgive me for..." When you have finished asking Jesus for forgiveness as your spouse, move to sit in chair B.

In chair B you will role-play being Jesus. Respond as you think Jesus would respond to your spouse's request for forgiveness. When you have finished forgiving your spouse as Jesus, move to chair A again.

In chair A, role-play your spouse responding to Jesus' forgiveness. When you finish, be still and experience what has transpired.[6]

By taking part in these four simple exercises, you have walked through forgiving yourself and your spouse from the past, and you have experienced the forgiveness of Jesus extended to both of you. These exercises *did not* require your spouse to be present or to repent or change so that you could release forgiveness to him or her.

With this experience behind you, it will be much easier for you to release current sins and extend forgiveness on a day-to-day basis. *Asking for and granting forgiveness are essential tools for maintaining a loving relationship.* We know that we are all going to sin. (Remember 1 Corinthians 13.) When we sin, acknowledge it as sin to your spouse and ask forgiveness. When asked for forgiveness, respond to your spouse as quickly as possible.

Ephesians 4:26 advises us: "Be angry, and do not sin: do not let the sun go down on your wrath" (NKJV). I think it is a good idea also not to let the sun go down on your sin. As much as possible, *do not go to bed without repairing anything that needs to be forgiven.*

It is time to break any old agreements with any previous unforgiveness. Pray this prayer aloud:

Jesus, I ask You to forgive me of any beliefs, attitudes, thoughts, or behaviors of unforgiveness toward my spouse. I confess these beliefs, attitudes, thoughts, or behaviors of unforgiveness as sin against You, my spouse, and myself. I break any agreements my mind, will, or emotions have had with unforgiveness, in Jesus' name.

MY COMMITMENT TO FORGIVENESS

It's time to make your love agreement to forgiveness.

LOVE AGREEMENT #3

WHEN I HAVE OFFENDED MY SPOUSE,
I WILL QUICKLY ASK FOR FORGIVENESS.
AND I WILL FORGIVE MY SPOUSE'S OFFENSES
IN MY HEART EVEN BEFORE BEING ASKED.

You are ready to embrace a new lifestyle of forgiving the sins of your spouse. Pray aloud:

In the name of Jesus, I make a love agreement to forgive my spouse. I command my mind, will, and emotions to create new beliefs, attitudes, thoughts, and behaviors to forgive my spouse. I also command my mind, will, and emotions to create new beliefs, attitudes, thoughts, and behaviors to help me to be honest about my own sins and to quickly and regularly ask my spouse to forgive me for my sins. I command this in the name of Jesus.

As in previous love agreements, we know the agreement is the first step in the process.

GOALS FOR FORGIVENESS

The next step to be successful in a love agreement is to make some goals that you can measure. Let's look at some possible goals for you to be successful in your love agreement of forgiveness.

Underline each of the following goals you are willing to make a commitment to keep, and for each goal you underline, fill in the specific behavior you will use to reach that goal.

- I will make a daily log of sins (which may be attitudes, behaviors, or the lack of) that I committed against my spouse.

  _____

- I will keep track daily of how long it takes me to ask for forgiveness of a sin I commit toward my spouse.

  _____

- I will make a plan to concentrate daily on overcoming one area of sin that causes me to wrong my spouse on a regular basis.

  _____

- I will keep a log indicating whether or not I went to sleep without asking forgiveness of my spouse of known sin.

  _____

- I will make a note at the end of the day of sins my spouse has made toward me. I will go into a room alone and not leave until I have forgiven my spouse of each sin, *without requiring my spouse to ask for forgiveness first.*

_____

- I will keep a log indicating whether or not I went to sleep without fully forgiving my spouse.

_____

- I will keep track of sins I commit throughout the day against myself. I will forgive myself for the sins I commit.

_____

MEASUREMENT AND ACCOUNTABILITY

The last step in a love agreement is measurement and accountability. As you did with the previous love agreements, devise a way to keep track of your progress and to assure your behavioral honesty in keeping your love agreement on forgiveness.

If you have asked a friend to be your accountability partner for these love agreements, set up regular times to go over your goals and measurements with them. Remember that *it is not your goal* to uncover your spouse's sins. Your spouse's sins are not the issue.

The goal is to increase your ability to keep your love agreement of forgiveness.

As forgiveness becomes a lifestyle pattern in your marriage, you will be able to be increasingly honest as you regularly ask forgiveness from your spouse for your own sinful actions. You will also be able to experience the joy of being able to love, even though you are married to a sinner—just as your spouse is also married to a sinner, which we all are. It's great to give that grace to others and allow them to be flawed and imperfect yet still so very much loved by God and by you. You deserve this lifestyle of freedom, freely loving your spouse!

Imagine how much better your marriage will be as day by day you give love and forgiveness to your spouse, even if they don't ask for it or repent. In time, as your spouse sees you smile instead of grimace when he or she wrongs you, your new attitude may cause a change in your spouse. After a while, your spouse might even stop some of those behaviors because it's just not fun anymore.

Like the other love agreements, forgiveness holds real power to affect your marriage positively. From this day forward, determine to be a great big forgiveness blessing to your spouse.

LOVE AGREEMENT #4

I will anticipate my spouse's spiritual,

emotional, physical, and material needs

and will do everything I can to meet them.

Chapter Six

Love Agreement #4:
SERVICE

On the night of Jesus' betrayal, Jesus took a towel and a basin of water and washed the feet of His disciples. (See John 13:1–17.) In Jesus' day, foot washing was a daily occurrence—*but it was the custom to have a household slave wash the feet of the guests.*

When Jesus and His disciples arrived at the upper room for their last meal together, none of the twelve disciples even considered making sure that everyone's feet were cleansed from the dust of the street. Jesus seized this opportunity to take a basin of water and wash His disciple's feet. This story is a great illustration of the call each of us has received to serve one another.

I recently saw another great illustration of Christian service. I arrived to pick my children up from a rehearsal for "The Thorn," a huge Easter production put on at the church with more than five hundred cast members. On this particular rehearsal day, prior to the rehearsal there had been a Veggie Tales preview for a new movie, with more than a thousand children present.

As I sat down to spend a few minutes writing while I waited for my children to finish their practice, I could see that snacks and drinks had been provided for the children watching the movie, since several people were hard at work cleaning up. Suddenly I saw Pastor Kevin, the children's pastor.

It was not unusual to see Pastor Kevin at the church at any time of the day because well over a thousand children had been entrusted to his care. He has several full-time and volunteer staff who report to him. But on this day when I saw Pastor Kevin at the church, he wasn't preaching, administrating, or any such thing. He was quietly using a large mop to clean up the floor from the mob of children who had been there earlier. You see, Pastor Kevin was just quietly serving.

Serving is a Christian virtue. There are many who strive *to lead*, but Christ calls us *to serve*. At one point, Jesus' disciples were arguing about which of them would be considered to be the greatest. When Jesus heard their dispute, He told them:

> The kings of the Gentiles exercise lordship over them, and those who exercise authority over them are called "benefactors." But not so among you; on the contrary, he who is greatest among you, let him be as the younger, and he who governs as he who serves. For who is greater, he who sits at the table, or he who serves? Is it not he who sits at the table? Yet I am among you as the One who serves.
>
> —LUKE 22:25–27, NKJV

God is looking for servants in the kingdom of God. In a Christian marriage this is also true of what God is looking for—a servant.

When we are called to marriage, we are called to servitude. We are saying "I do" to serving the other person all the days of our lives. Some of us have it backward—we think our spouse is supposed to be our servant. I'm sorry, but that is not what God intended. We are both called to serve each other.

There are several areas of need where you must learn to serve your spouse in marriage. It is a good idea to discuss these various areas to give you a chance to evaluate how you are serving your spouse in each of these areas.

SPIRITUAL SERVICE

Your spouse needs you to serve him or her spiritually. You can serve your spouse spiritually by being spiritually strong, praying, studying the Word, and developing a circle of good Christian friends.

Your spouse needs you to serve by being his or her best intercessor. At the very least, pray daily for your spouse. Care enough about your spouse's spiritual growth to ask about the spiritual lessons he or she is learning. Discuss his or her daily Bible study, and be interested in his or her one-on-one relationship with Christ.

Your spouse also needs you to serve by being faithful in a local church. Maintain a consistent and positive attitude about your local church and give financially to it as well. The local church is the best way to grow and practice your faith. Being planted firmly in a local church will encourage both of you to be rooted in God and His people as you go through all the various trials and seasons of life.

Your spouse also needs your servant's heart spiritually as you serve your children. Many parents are not intentionally involved in their children's spiritual growth. But you can be. Serve your children's spirit by praying with them, reading the Word to them, getting them involved in the local church, and seeing that they have Christian friends.

EMOTIONAL SERVICE

Everybody needs an emotional cheerleader, someone who encourages you and lifts your spirit when you are feeling low. To serve another person emotionally does not require the ability to solve problems—it just requires your presence and support.

An emotional servant invites his or her spouse to discover hidden feelings so he or she can understand what is going on inside. An emotional servant doesn't shame his or her spouse for incongruent feelings and doesn't bring those feelings back up later to belittle that person.

Be committed to becoming your spouse's emotional servant. Keep yourself emotionally fit so that you know and understand the feelings you are experiencing within yourself. Be vulnerable yourself so your spouse will feel safe sharing his or her feelings with you.

Above all, protect your spouse's heart. What your spouse shares with you is shared in utmost confidence—don't share it with friends, parents, or siblings. It is to be kept just between the two of you.

PHYSICAL SERVICE

A very important area of your spouse's life is the physical body. Some spouses are great about taking care of their bodies, and others are . . . let's say, less responsible.

One important area of physical service is exercise. Now you can't abruptly say, "Hey, honey, let me drop you off at the gym." But you can invite your spouse to begin attending a gym with you. If you are parents of young children, you can join a gym that has child care and *go to the gym together*. You can also suggest going for walks together. It's important that your spouse is healthy.

Some women feel more comfortable in a women's only gym. If so, serve your wife by doing whatever is necessary to provide her with the time to go to the gym. Exercise is important in every marriage, and Lisa and I have made it a priority in ours. We regularly serve each other by providing each other with opportunities to exercise. Our family members do not sit around watching television in the evening, and we don't play video games. We may watch an occasional video, but we are more likely to play games, hike, walk the dog, or do something to provide our bodies with an opportunity to exercise.

Exercise is not the only area where your spouse needs your service. Food is also another area where service is important. Obesity is rampant in the church. This may be a very sensitive area, because so many Americans have little self-control with food.

But there are many ways where you can provide service to your spouse in the area of nutrition. Here is how Lisa serves our family in the area of food. She doesn't buy candy, cookies, or a lot of sugary snacks. She makes healthy homemade snacks for our family. She provides us with healthy options like fruit to eat. She prepares dinner early so we are not eating late and going straight to bed.

We also serve each other by getting on the scale daily. This way I know if I have to be careful in eating that day or need to add some additional exercise. If I know which way my weight is going, then I can change. Our bodies are a gift we give to God and our spouse.

I really appreciate the way Lisa serves me physically. She looks as great now as she did twenty years ago and still wears the same size after the childbearing years. Part of serving your spouse is trying to be reasonably fit. When you don't exercise, your stress accumulates, and you can become less fun for everyone around you.

Material Service

We live in a material world. We all need clothes, shoes, furniture, beauty products, and an endless list of other legitimate needs and wants. We can also serve our spouses by creating wealth.

In America both men and women can create wealth. Even in ancient days when women were not valued, they did this. The Proverbs 31 woman was creating wealth. She had a real estate venture and a retail venture, and she still kept her family well taken care of. If both you and your spouse are creating wealth, you will be able to save for college expenses and retirement more easily and will have more to give to advance the kingdom of God.

Creating wealth is only one part of serving your spouse materially.

You must also manage your resources well. I know millionaires who go bankrupt. It's not only what you make; it's what you do with it. Have an intelligent plan for money that you can agree on. Never live on 100 percent of what you earn. Have a very conservative debt policy.

As a Christian, I would suggest tithing. Almost every couple I have seen over the years with money problems were people who did not tithe. I have tithed ever since I was saved. More than twenty years later, I can honestly say that I believe the blessing of God is on our material lives due to being obedient in this area.

If you are serving each other by creating wealth, managing your income, and tithing to the Lord, when your spouse desires something of material value, and that item is reasonable, you will probably be able to fulfill that desire, whether it be a necessity or just a toy. Serving each other materially feels great!

SEXUAL SERVICE

Sex is one of the greatest gifts God gives to a married couple. Sex is great. Sex is also a place where your spouse needs your service. In this area, your spouse is totally dependant upon your Christlikeness. If one person in a marriage relationship is sexually self-centered, it will cause pain for the spouse and will bring harm to the marriage relationship.

Serve your spouse sexually by guarding your sexuality, including your forms of entertainment, conversations with others, and what you view on the Internet. Your sex organ belongs to God and to your spouse, not to yourself. (See 1 Corinthians 7:1–5.)

You should not be entertaining lustful thoughts about others (Exod. 20:17; Matt. 5:28). That means absolutely no pornography. Take the first step to healing yourself sexually so that you can serve your spouse.

Sexual abuse also is an issue that impacts some Christian men and women. If you are included in this number, then you will need to heal this area of your life in order to serve your spouse. I recommend that you do the Cleanse the Temple exercise described earlier in this book for any past sexual perpetrators, so that you can serve your spouse sexually.

You and your spouse will probably have very different sexual preferences and desires. If these differences are causing problems in your relationship, I strongly recommend that you read my book *Intimacy: A 100-Day Guide to Lasting Relationships*.

You can walk in agreement as to what is in your sexual garden of preferences. You can serve your spouse by honoring his or her sexual personality and by not trying to mold him or her into your own image.

Serve your spouse sexually by saving some physical energy for your spouse and by making sure the bedroom door is locked so you will not be interrupted. Avoid overworking or overcleaning, because both can wear you out. Pace yourself. If you have medical or emotional issues regarding your sexuality, be prompt in attempting to resolve these issues.

SERVING IN AREAS OF ENTERTAINMENT AND FUN

Everyone needs fun and entertainment in their lives. Hopefully you didn't marry your spouse to bore them to death. Do your best to serve your spouse in the area of fun.

It may be as simple as rotating weekly dates so that both of you are having fun. Dating is critical to a healthy marriage. Having regular fun is important. These events will, of course, need to be planned, and you can start serving your spouse by having ideas to go places on the weekend. Vacations are important as well. I strongly encourage couples to make vacations fun and relaxing. Consider that one of you might think a fun vacation would involve excitement and risk, and the other may want a quiet, relaxing rest.

Serve your spouse by acknowledging how your spouse relaxes. Make sure both of you are getting a fair shake on your dates and vacations. If you are always doing what *you* want to do, you are not serving your spouse. Work together to serve each other by including forms of entertainment that are satisfying and fulfilling to both of you.

HOUSEHOLD SERVICE

Household issues in a marriage are very important. This is where the rubber meets the road regarding serving one another. But it is easy to find ways to serve your spouse in the home, because there are always helpful things for both of you to do around the house.

Begin your service to your spouse by making absolutely sure that you are doing at least the agreed-upon portion of what needs to be done. Not doing what you have agreed to do will create legitimate resentment in your relationship.

Serve your spouse by occasionally taking on a chore that your spouse normally does—and do it well. Just as there is neither *male* nor *female* in Christ, there are no chores that are masculine or feminine (Gal. 3:28).

You can serve in any area of household duty. Be an aggressive servant. Stay ahead of the game in the household area. When you see towels or laundry on the floor, pick them up. When you find dirty dishes in the sink, wash them. Just dig in and do it. Don't have a keeping-score attitude; have a winning-score attitude. As a Christian servant you don't want to have a "getting even" or "I did this, and you do that" mentality. *Out-serve your spouse regularly*—doing more than he or she does. Usually it doesn't even take that much time.

Sit down together and develop a project list upon which you both agree. Then, systematically get it done. Don't say you are too busy to help. Trust me, I am a busy guy, so I know you have no excuse. For me, folding laundry is a way to serve my wife and knowing whether the dishes in the dishwasher are clean or dirty is one of my ways to romance her. I don't consider myself too good to serve my wife, for she is a queen of God's, and our family is royalty. Serving her is my duty and my delight.

I keep up with the odd jobs and "honey dos." I know this is a way of loving Lisa, so it's no big deal. Besides, it's fun to serve your spouse around the house—changing light bulbs, taking out garbage, wiping kitchen counters down, putting dishes in the dishwasher, or putting them away. This is nothing for a servant of the living God.

It feels good to serve your spouse in the various areas of his or her life. I believe that you can actually increase your love for your spouse by serving. A servant's heart makes you feel good by doing helpful things for the people you love. In my experience, it also is a tangible way for them to feel your love.

I feel loved when Lisa changes a light bulb. Why? Because that's usually my job, so when she does it in service to me, it blesses me. We both win when we serve each other. The love agreement of service takes time and energy, but it's fun when you're doing it in the right spirit for someone you love.

Before you make your commitment to service, take the time to break your old agreement to be served, and make one instead to serve. Pray this prayer aloud:

Jesus, I ask forgiveness for the sin of being selfish and my lack of serving my spouse. I command any agreements of this ungodly attitude to be broken in my mind, will, and emotions. I command the attitudes, beliefs, or behaviors that have been selfish and not serving to my spouse to be broken in the name of Jesus.

That's terrific! The first step of making a love agreement is to break away from previous agreements that are opposed to your new path of life.

My Commitment to Service

Now, let's officially make a love agreement for service.

I WILL ANTICIPATE MY SPOUSE'S SPIRITUAL,
EMOTIONAL, PHYSICAL, AND MATERIAL NEEDS AND
WILL DO EVERYTHING I CAN TO MEET THEM.

If you are ready to make this commitment, pray this prayer aloud:

Jesus, I officially make a love agreement to serve my spouse fully. I command my mind, will, and emotions to create new attitudes, beliefs, and behaviors to serve my spouse. I am in agreement to out-serve my spouse all the days of my marriage. I now make this agreement, in the name of Jesus Christ.

This might be a landmark agreement for some of you. Serving is a heart attitude that will continue to grow as you apply this love agreement on a regular basis.

SETTING YOUR GOALS

Now that you have made a love agreement to serve, move on into the next step of setting goals for yourself. In the sections below you will be able to set goals in each of the different areas for service that we covered in this chapter. You may already be providing outstanding service to your spouse in some of these areas, but there are probably others where you need to give some additional focus. So pick an area you would like to zero in on, and make some goals.

In each area, underline the goals you are willing to make a commitment to keep, and for each goal you underline, fill in the specific behavior you will use to reach that goal.

GOALS FOR SPIRITUAL SERVICE

• I will choose a specific time to pray daily for my spouse.

_____

• I will schedule a regular time of prayer with my spouse.

_____

• I will schedule a regular time for reading the Word together.

_____

- I will invite my spouse into a time of worship together.

  _____

- I will attend church regularly and be involved in church life.

  _____

- I will invite my spouse to share with me what God is teaching him or her, and how.

  _____

- I will nurture the spiritual lives of my children.

  _____

GOALS FOR EMOTIONAL SERVICE

- I will give encouragement regularly.

  _____

- I will ask my spouse to share his or her feelings and will listen carefully.

  _____

- I will "listen" to the nonverbal feelings that my spouse expresses and ask my spouse to talk about those feelings.

  _____

- I will keep myself aware of what I am feeling.

  _____

- When my spouse is sharing a childhood story or a current event, I will ask him or her to express his or her feelings about it.

  _____

- When making decisions, I will invite my spouse to express his or her feelings about my decision.

  _____

GOALS FOR PHYSICAL SERVICE

- I am committed to exercise ____ times a week.

  _____

- I will invite my spouse to walk, bike, or do another exercise together.

  _____

- I will be wise about my use of caffeine or sugar.

  _____

- I will make healthy choices about the things I eat.

  _____

- I will pray for any physical issues my spouse is dealing with.

  _____

GOALS FOR MATERIAL SERVICE

- I will evaluate my current plans for the creation of wealth.

  _____

- I will evaluate my current budgeting decisions.

  _____

- I will evaluate my current plan for saving money.

  _____

- I will evaluate my current plans for saving college funds for our children's education.

  _____

- I will evaluate my current financial goals for retirement.

  _____

- I will evaluate my current philosophy and practice of debt.

  _____

- I will evaluate my current commitment to tithing.

  _____

- I will invite my spouse's insights into the evaluation processes in my above goals.

  _____

- I have set a goal to provide a material item for my spouse for which he or she has expressed a desire.

  _____

GOALS FOR SEXUAL SERVICE

- I will thank God for my spouse's sexuality and sexual personality.

  _____

- I will practice acceptance and celebration of my spouse's sexuality.

  _____

- I will intentionally try to please my spouse sexually.

  _____

- I will touch my spouse intentionally in nonsexual ways.

  _____

- I will not ask my spouse to respond sexually in ways that are uncomfortable to him or her.

  _____

- I will plan my day to have energy for sexual intimacy.

  _____

- I will make attempts at having some special sexual encounters.

  _____

GOALS FOR ENTERTAINMENT AND FUN

- I will attempt to date my spouse weekly or biweekly.

  _____

- I will occasionally choose an activity that would be fun for my spouse and do it with a good attitude.

  _____

- I will discuss vacation plans with my spouse so that the needs we both have can be met.

_____

- I will create a list of enjoyable things to both of us and will find ways to schedule them into our regular lifestyle.

_____

- I will create a budget for regular dating and special vacations.

_____

- I will schedule a getaway weekend for just my spouse and me.

_____

GOALS FOR HOUSEHOLD SERVICE

- I will make a list of household projects that are my responsibility to complete.

_____

- I will monitor my success in my agreed-upon household responsibilities.

_____

- Once a ___ I will plan to do one of my spouse's chores.

  _____

- I will accomplish a specific household project ___ times per month.

  _____

- I will pick up around the house more than my spouse and with a good attitude.

  _____

- I will thank my spouse for his or her work around the house.

  _____

MEASURE YOUR PROGRESS

The love agreement of service is a very practical agreement. To be successful, this service agreement, like other agreements, is best when your progress is measured. So pick a goal and then create your measure for assessing your progress on serving your spouse.

It is best if you stick to one goal at a time to be successful. You'll want to stay focused to achieve one goal and then move on to the next service goal.

Meet with your accountability partner on a regular basis, and go over your goals. You will learn a lot about yourself as you attempt to serve your spouse. Try to keep the learning focused on your side of the fence.

Avoid developing the opinion that your spouse is selfish and ungrateful for the ways you serve. With that attitude, you will not be able to keep your love agreement to serve. Instead, you will begin to feel like a victim.

When I was getting my education, it didn't take long for me to understand that I got a grade for each test that I took. If I studied, I would get a good grade. If I didn't study, the grade was certainly not good. I did not have to concern myself with a classmate who did not study and therefore received a worse grade than mine. Their grade was not my issue. Just so, do not be tempted to focus on your spouse's service to you—whether it be good or bad. Your spouse may have his or her own issues to work through; we all do.

Look at it this way: has your focus on your spouse's issues ever made a difference in the past? Probably not!

But as you serve, and, maybe, out-serve your spouse, the dynamics in your marriage will begin to change. Change is usually a good thing. Serve fully, and keep your eyes on Jesus, not on your spouse. Then you will feel His smile at the end of the day and hear Him say, "Well done, good and faithful servant" (Matt. 25:21, NKJV).

LOVE AGREEMENT #5

I will not act or speak in a way that

demeans, ridicules, or embarrasses

my spouse.

Chapter Seven

Love Agreement #5:
RESPECT

It was a typical Sunday for Louis and Rose. They hustled the kids to get dressed and soon were on their way out the door for the drive to church. They sent the kids off to their Sunday school classrooms and hurried to the sanctuary for a great worship service and sermon from their pastor. Soon they were driving home from church. As they entered the house, they observed a great mess. No, it wasn't what you think—no one broke into their home. It was just the mess they left in their rush to get ready for church.

Rose launched the first comment, "Louis, help pick up this mess."

Defensively, Louis shouted back, "It's not my mess. I picked up all morning while you were doing your hair."

"That's ridiculous," she retorted. "How could you have picked up when the place looks like this?"

They continued to banter back and forth as their children, who just heard great Bible stories at church, heard their parents attack each other.

Karl and Julie had been married for just a few months when they entered counseling with me. Julie complained that since their marriage, Karl had continuously been putting her down. "I can't seem to do anything right," she told me. "Not the laundry, cooking, sex, money—nothing at all. I don't want to live in a marriage where I have to hear him correcting me all the time. I hate it. I hate it." As she talked, tears flowed down her face in front of Karl and me.

Both couples, Louis and Rose and Karl and Julie, shared a similar issue. They both lacked a fundamental respect for each other. As I counsel with couples like Julie and Karl, they often admit that they saw their parents act disrespectfully to one another, and they just thought it was normal to be disrespectful to your spouse.

Others explain that they arrived at the place where Louis and Rose had arrived after a slow erosion of respect that occurred over time. Louis and Rose didn't fall out of love; *they just fell out of respect for each other.*

I have discovered that there are several types of "games" of disrespect that couples may play in a marriage. The first game has become known as the "One Up" game. It's a game couples play when each spouse wants to be the winner or the one on top. Either spouse can initiate the game, but once the game starts, it's off to the races.

There are no rules to the "One Up" game, just a winner and a loser. Once you start, you can bring up negative history about your spouse, attack your spouse's character, gender, family of origin, or do anything else that will prove that you are one up on your spouse.

Another game some couples play is "Mr. Superior or Mrs. Superior." In this game, one person assumes an emotionally based position of superiority. That person may back it up by age, education, or life experiences, but somehow he or she is superior to his or her spouse. Couples playing this game don't even argue much; they are simply right because of who they are.

In each of these games, one spouse projects a false self-image, one that is not human, not flawed, not a sinner, just simply wonderful all the time. These false self-types usually disrespect their less-than-wonderful spouses. It always amazes me how these perfect people can pick such terrible sinners for spouses. When someone is being disrespectful to his/her spouse due to a false self-image, it's difficult to get very far with that person in counseling because he or she is not being honest about himself or herself.

CORE BELIEFS OF A DISRESPECTFUL SPOUSE

There are core beliefs that even a disrespectful spouse holds as important. In this section I am including some core beliefs for you to read and apply to yourself. I know you'll be tempted to look at your spouse, but please don't do this. Knowing your spouse's defects will not help you to change personally. Remember that when *you* change, this change also influences your marriage.

"I have a right to criticize."

A disrepecter believes that just because he can see a weakness, deficiency, or a less than wonderful quality about his spouse, he has the right to highlight this deficiency to his spouse. He almost feels like it is his duty to share those faults with his spouse regularly, as if sharing the criticism will greatly benefit his spouse and help her to grow.

In my professional experience, a disrepecter, in general, is not a very good prayer warrior. The weaknesses you see in your spouse should be covered in your prayers before you bring it to your spouse—if it is ever to be brought to him or her at all.

"My perceptions are truth."

A disrepecter has unquestionable authority. Her perceptions are absolute. She has innate powers to interpret your thoughts, motives, and beliefs at all times. What you were truly thinking or feeling is not real; only what she thinks you were thinking and the things she thinks motivated your actions are the real truth.

This disrepecter will spend countless hours convincing you of "what you really meant" or "why you really did such and such." If you are in a marriage with a disrepecter, no doubt you have spent many long nights in heated discussions.

"It's always your fault."

This core belief is steeped in denial. Anyone who believes that he never has anything to do with the less-than-positive interactions in a marriage is plainly and simply *in denial.* This disrepecter lives in a myopic relationship with self. He believes he is always the "right" one. If there is anything negative that must be dealt with, it has to be someone else's fault, because he is wonderful. My experience is that this disrespecter usually has secrets that he feels very badly about, which is why making any further mistakes makes him feel worse and more hopeless.

"I'm just having fun."

This disrespecter couches her disrespect and superiority in humor: "You know I don't really mean it." But she says it often enough to make you wonder what she was really thinking. If she puts you down in front of others and gets other disrespecters to laugh as well, then "it's just having fun."

Usually these disrespecters are thin-skinned. If you really turn the tables and move others to laugh at them, they usually get mad. Then this disrespect isn't fun anymore; you're just being mean.

"I'm angry, too bad."

This disrespecter's core belief is that if he is mad, there are no rules. To shred you into little pieces or to demean you is perfectly permissible behavior. If he pushes you to fight back or cry, it's just too bad for you. You deserve the bad treatment because "I'm mad, and I need someone else to project my pain on to."

"Your heart has no value."

This core belief is hard to understand if you are a person who values the other person's feelings. This disrespecter truly doesn't care about what you feel or think. To her, it is much more important that you capitulate or comply with her agenda or belief than she with yours. It's more important that you obey what she says than who you are. Being heard is irrelevant; this ship is going in her direction. Therefore, her perspective is, "Get on or get out of the way!"

Clearly, being a disrespecter is so contrary to the heart and nature of Christ. Take a moment and think through the issue of love and respect. God is all-knowing. He is all-powerful, and He really is God of heaven and earth. He not only came to earth, but He came to earth as one of His creations—a man. He came to try and teach us. He died, rose again, and is coming back for us. He not only loves us, but He also respects the value He has given to us.

Now, remember this: God didn't come to do all this just for you; *He did it for your spouse, too.* Your spouse is beloved by God. Christ died for your spouse and respects him or her. He listens to your spouse's heart, his or her less-than-logical discussions, and He does it respectfully.

A *respecter* relates more from a life and relationship perspective, a totally different perspective than the one a disrespecter has. A respecter understands the definition of respect. *To respect* is "to give honor or preference toward another person."

Most of us have people to whom we give honor or preference. These people may be our pastors or someone much older and more successful than ourselves. Most of us would honor the president of the United States, a famous actor or celebrity, or even our own children. If you knew the child of someone famous, you might give honor to that person because of his or her father's status.

Recently I had the privilege to host the *Praise the Lord* show on TBN. Although I have hosted *Praise the Lord* before, this was extra special because the show was solely focused on marriage. Some of the best Christian writers and counselors were on this show, including one of the fathers of the Christian marriage movement, Dr. Gary Smalley. Greg Smalley, his son, was also on the show that night. I could feel myself giving honor to Greg Smalley because he was the son of someone I honored.

I think you know where I am going. If God, who is King of all kings of all time, had a child, you would honor that child, wouldn't you? That child through Christ Jesus is your spouse. Respecting your spouse is the beginning of this love agreement.

CORE BELIEFS OF A RESPECTER

Respecters also have a set of core beliefs. These beliefs are quite different from those of the disrespecter, which we discussed earlier.

We are equal.

A respecter comes into marriage with an idea that his spouse is totally equal in value. His spouse can reason and have a different perspective, but there is still equality. The value of a respecter isn't based on gender, success, or education; it's based on the blood of Jesus Christ. This core of equality allows the respecter to hear his spouse fully because he believes that if he doesn't listen carefully, he may miss something valuable.

Hearts are valuable.

The respecter not only wants to know the mind of her spouse, she also wants to know how he feels. The respecter is focused on connecting heart to heart. She would consider that the person who attempted to rule over another person's heart in order to get to a goal or just to be right was very gross and immature. Staying in a connected relationship is more valuable to the respecter than closing the deal. The respecter values the person over outcomes.

Truth is a journey.

The respecter truly knows and believes in his heart that he does not know all truth at all times. He knows that God distributes truth. He knows his spouse has some pieces of truth, and that together they may or may not have all the truth they need to move through an issue. There is humility in the heart of a respecter to seek truth and not presume he knows truth.

No emotion justifies rudeness.

A respecter is not perfect. She has emotions as well. She can dislike others, become hurt, or get mad like the rest of us. She just doesn't allow herself to do it! The bottom line is that it's not right to be rude or unkind. It would hurt her so much more to act like a disrespecter than just to be quiet and try to be gracious. The respecter knows what my pastor, Ted Haggard, tells us all the time: "Have manners and be nice."

We are allowed to be different.

Being different, seeing things differently, and even having different outcomes is normal for the respecter. What would you expect from any two people who have different life experiences, priorities, and education, not to mention genders?

To expect two people to agree on everything or think that one of them is always right is absolutely insane thinking to the respecter. It just doesn't make sense to believe in sameness when God intentionally and expertly made us entirely different from one another. For the respecter, it is totally acceptable to disagree—we will do that throughout our entire lives, anyway. Navigating differences respectfully is expected, but to assume agreement isn't even in the psyche of a respecter.

Your spouse is by far the most important person in your life. You can evaluate yourself by now. Are you more closely aligned to the core beliefs of a *disrespecter* or a *respecter*? Take a moment and really think about this.

At a core level *you know that it is best to treat your spouse regularly with respect.* You also know innately that it is best to honor your spouse with your words and with your actions. You also know that *it takes some effort not to demean, ridicule, or embarrass your spouse.*

Respecting another person as God respects you is encouraging that person to operate in his or her strengths. Show respect for your spouse by encouraging him or her to focus on the gifts God has given to him or her. Show your appreciation for those gifts.

Of course you can see your spouse's weaknesses, but *respect comes alongside those weaknesses in a supportive manner that encourages your spouse to mature.* As parents, many of us see the weaknesses of our children. They may take after our spouse or us or have their own unique weaknesses. Hopefully, we don't come along and demean or criticize them. Rather we respect them and offer to help them grow out of their weaknesses.

My daughter, Hadassah, just started Tae-Kwon-Do this year. Her brother started almost five years ago and has very advanced belts. He taught her the first white belt form before her first class. It took almost three months until she tested for her first belt change. I didn't shame, her but I finally asked her what the issue was.

I discovered that she didn't want to test in front of all the other students and their parents. She had some fear of this. I came alongside Hadassah and told her, "Listen, if you overcome this fear by the next testing, I will give you a certain amount of money to put in your bank." Money is very valuable for Hadassah. Needless to say, she promptly took her test and received her new yellow belt.

Just as you respect your children and help them to mature out of their weaknesses, you should also respect your spouse in his or her weakness. In God's sight, we are all infants, each created differently. I encourage you to enjoy each other's differences. Respect allows the independent and different developments of a spouse's interest and gifts. A disrespecter wants to control and stifle his or her spouse.

Give respectful space to your spouse to grow and become who he or she is in the image of Christ.

Respect and disrespect can happen in an instant. I know instantly when I have shown disrespect to Lisa. Perhaps I didn't let her finish a sentence or thought, or I discounted what she had to say without supporting how she came to her conclusions. In my disrespect I may tell her why she did that thing and point out her track record with that weakness in an attempt to play the "One Up" game.

You see, I am human, too. Respect, like all the love agreements, must exhibit growth by changing our current behavior.

Respect is something we give away. Keep on practicing the giving of respect. Let it flow from God through you, ultimately arriving in your spouse's heart.

Before you make your love agreement of respect, stop to break any agreement you have had of being disrespectful to your spouse. Pray this prayer aloud:

Lord Jesus, I confess all thoughts, feelings, beliefs, attitudes, and behaviors of disrespect toward my spouse as absolute sin. I confess it always was, always is, and always will be a sin to disrespect Your child, my spouse. I ask You to break any strongholds of disrespect, whether they be in my mind, my will, or my emotions. Break them off my spirit, soul, and body. I no longer agree in any way to disrespect Your child, my spouse.

My Commitment to Respect

Congratulations! You have taken the first big step. Now make your love agreement to respect.

I WILL NOT ACT OR SPEAK IN A WAY
THAT DEMEANS, RIDICULES,
OR EMBARRASSES MY SPOUSE.

Pray this prayer aloud:

In the name of Jesus, I command my mind, will, and emotions to create new thoughts, beliefs, attitudes, and behaviors of respect toward my spouse. Today I officially make a love agreement to respect and love my spouse in the name of Jesus.

Setting Your Goals

As we have in each love agreement, we need to discuss some goals to grow in respect. These goals will assist you in achieving your ultimate goal of keeping your love agreement of respect. Underline the goals you are willing to make a commitment to keep, and for each goal you underline, fill in the specific behavior you will use to reach that goal.

GOALS FOR RESPECTING MY SPOUSE

- I will let my spouse complete his or her sentences.

  _____

- I will listen to the thoughts my spouse expresses enough to repeat what he or she is saying before I make comments.

  _____

- I will ask my spouse to explain how he or she came to those conclusions.

  _____

- I will agree with my spouse to pray over a matter before we make any decisions.

  _____

- I will forgo my idea or choice in deference to his or her idea or choice.

  _____

- I will write down five things I respect about my spouse and make efforts to communicate my respect to him or her about these qualities regularly.

  _____

- I will ask for my spouse's opinion about those things I normally decide about myself.

  _____

- I will ask for forgiveness if I disrespect my spouse, even if he or she does not notice my disrespect.

  _____

- I will encourage my spouse in an area of strength or interest.

  _____

- I will make affirming, respectful comments intentionally and regularly in front of my children.

  _____

- I will make affirming, respectful comments intentionally about my spouse in front of our friends.

  _____

MEASURE FOR SUCCESS

Now that you have chosen your goals, it is time to create a way to measure your progress for the goals you have chosen to facilitate progress in your love agreement of respect. Whether it's a stick-up note, a check-off list, or a spreadsheet, make something tangible to report your growth.

The last step in any love agreement is accountability. Once you have connected with your accountability partner, establish the frequency with which you will meet. Also establish exactly what your goals are for your love agreement of respect.

Remember that respect is more often *caught* than *taught*. As you actively respect your spouse, expect some unique and even inquiring responses as to why you are acting differently. That's a good sign that your respect is having an impact.

Like all the love agreements, the love agreement of respect is powerful. To be respected, heard, and affirmed can be a system-changing type of encounter. Be prepared that in time your spouse may actually hear you and begin to mirror back the respect you are giving to him or her. Give it a try. After all, isn't everyone looking for just a little respect?

LOVE AGREEMENT #6

I will be kind to my spouse, eliminating

any trace of meanness from my behavior

and speech.

Chapter Eight

Love Agreement #6:
KINDNESS

James had a really hard day at work. The computer program he had been working on for weeks wasn't running properly again. His team leader and boss were sharing some of their concerns about James' abilities today. Tired after putting in his fiftieth twelve-hour day in a row, he headed home.

There was an accident on the highway that stopped all traffic, and no one was going anywhere for the next hour. Horns were honking, people were bickering at each other, and when traffic began to move, it was slow going. When he arrived home, James eagerly opened the door to see Fran, who was four months pregnant with their first child.

"I hope you're not going to work all hours of the day and night when the baby is born," she blurted out as she headed toward the refrigerator to grab a plate that was prepared two hours earlier. James was speechless as he walked by the baby books she had been reading throughout the day. He was desperately in need of something, but he couldn't put his finger exactly on what it was.

Charlotte, a homeschool mom of four children, also had a very rough day. It started just ten minutes after her husband had left for an important meeting in a city an hour away. Timmy, the third son, was throwing everything up and had a high fever.

Breakfast was served and cleaned up; school started for the other three children, grading assignments followed, lunch came and went, and more schoolwork continued. Charlotte was preparing dinner when her husband, Dan, came in the door, "Wow, it looks like a disaster happened here. What did you all do today?" he said smiling.

Charlotte did not have a return smile for Dan. She became defensive as she set the table for dinner. Charlotte also needed something but felt too overwhelmed to communicate whatever it was to Dan.

Both James and Charlotte needed something, all right; they both needed an act of kindness. James needed a kiss and hug and a "Boy, am I glad to see you, you hard-working man" from his wife.

Charlotte needed Dan to see her overwhelmed state and just pitch right in. For Charlotte, Dan's triumphant entry would have gone something like "Wow, I am glad I'm home to help; it looks like you could use some support" as he kissed her, grabbed the boys, and, after giving them a hug, gave them assignments to help Mom out, too.

Kindness is something your spouse needs daily. Your spouse may not even know he or she needs it or even how to ask for it. It is just very obvious when kindness has run out.

Kindness is the oil in a relationship. Let me explain this. Most men know that the parts in an engine move very fast. Most of us feel that our lives are like that also. We are continually working hard, chauffeuring kids, volunteering at church, helping out friends, and tending to the house.

Oil is what keeps the engine lubricated to reduce friction, overheating, and the eventual locking up of the engine. Like motor oil, kindness lubricates your marriage relationship. It is the random and intentional acts of kindness in a marriage that ease the frictions in life. It's the help, the smile, and the kind words that make the responsibilities of life more tolerable and significant. It's the "thanks for taking the garbage out" that makes taking the garbage down the driveway for the 1,329th time more meaningful. The fact that someone cares enough to notice and say *thank you* makes life just a little bit easier.

Think about this for a moment. When your spouse has been kind to you, what is your immediate reaction? Don't you feel more warm and friendly toward your spouse? Don't you feel just a little closer and more affirmed and appreciated by your spouse than just prior to these acts of kindness?

Of course you feel all those things, and much more. We are all human, and we all need kindness, whether we know it or not. Human beings can feel the lack of kindness in a relationship. Some feel it in measurement of a few days. For others it takes a little longer to feel the deprivation of kindness.

Just stop and think about the last week or so. How does your spouse feel about the acts of kindness he or she received from you during this period of time? Does your spouse feel satiated by the acts of kindness received from you? Would he or she say they had some kindness shown to him or her from you *but not enough*? Or would your spouse feel starved?

Kindness is a fruit of the Spirit. It's a fruit we all need to eat. There is something special in the nutrients of this fruit that makes anyone feel special.

Stop for a moment and recall some act of kindness shown to you. How did you feel? Did you feel cared for, important, and special? When you eat the fruit of kindness, it is so sweet to the soul. Do you remember the last act of kindness your spouse did for you? Do you remember how it made you feel?

You have the power of kindness locked inside of you through the Spirit of God. As a Christian, kindness is within you, and it wants to get out. Remember that with any act of kindness you show to your spouse, you are planting the seed of kindness inside his or her soul. In time, the seed you planted will eventually grow.

What will that seed become? It will become a tree with the fruit of kindness. You will get to eat the fruits of your planting. You may be reaping a plentiful harvest because of your continual planting and reaping. Or, are you honest enough to admit that you will probably reap a very small harvest?

Any day is a good day for planting kindness. As in the other love agreements, the love agreement of kindness does not depend on your spouse. Even the strongest will is not more powerful than the power of the seed or the biblical principle of sowing and reaping.

I live in Colorado, where we often see a peculiar sight. At times while hiking or driving, we will see huge trees that have grown right through rocks and boulders. It's amazing to see the power of a seed become far greater than the power of these rocks.

TYPES OF KINDNESS

There are several kinds of kindness that should be a part of your love agreement. *Kindness is a pivotal behavior in the love agreements.* Kindness is caring for a spouse with great gentleness and without a trace of meanness. Kindness is a meek person who has strength but chooses to use it in a gentle manner toward the people he or she loves. Gentleness is a directed strength with the sole purpose to support, encourage, or strengthen our spouses.

You were given the strength to be kind in order to strengthen the spirit, soul, and person of your spouse. When kindness is added to your love agreements, you become an empowerer of your spouse.

Your spouse will go from strength to strength because you are using kindness to encourage them to fly. David, one of the greatest Bible characters and a friend of God, referred not to God's power or wisdom, but rather to His gentleness as the thing that made Him great. (See 2 Samuel 18:5; Psalm 18:35.) As we are kind and gentle in spirit, it can help our spouses become great.

Spoken kindness

The first seed of kindness we can sow into the heart of our spouse is words of kindness. Start responding kindly to your spouse. Often, out of laziness or familiarity, we begin to be gruff, sarcastic, or demeaning in our responses to normal questions. Our answers seem sharp instead of seasoned with grace.

Responding kindly is a powerful tool. Respond as though every question your spouse asks you is an intelligent question. Respond as though you always, and I mean always, have time to listen fully and answer any question your spouse asks. Try it—responding kindly can make your spouse wonder what has gotten into you.

Another form of spoken kindness is expressed by the tone we use when we speak. It's possible, technically, to never say a wrong thing, yet communicate an unkind attitude when we talk. Remember, you will sow what you reap. This is a lesson I am still learning, because, like you, I haven't arrived here yet either. I can choose the spirit in which I speak to my wife. This is an area I have to stay focused on to have a kind disposition when I am communicating to my precious Lisa.

A third form of kind communication is speaking kind words. Notice the little and large things your spouse does for you. Make kind comments to your spouse in front of your friends and children. Always thank your spouse when he or she is serving you in some manner. Saying "Thank you, honey, for getting the butter; that was kind of you" can highlight the kindness he or she just showed to you. Responding like that is better than merely saying, "Thanks, honey." Both responses are adequate, but the first comment crystallizes to your spouse that you actually see his or her acts of kindness. Your spouse will eventually believe what you say—that he or she is kind.

I want my spouse, Lisa, to believe that I believe she is kind. If she believes she is kind, she will behave with even more kindness. I know Lisa believes she is kind because she constantly sows kindness into my life.

I can tell you that a kind response makes me feel respected, even if my ideas are not fully thought through. A thank you from her makes me want to do more for her. An acknowledgement of my kindness makes me feel like she sees me and loves me. Spoken kindness is so powerful to people, especially when it comes from their spouse.

I don't know if you realize this or not, but next to God, you are the loudest and most consistent voice your spouse will hear throughout his or her life. Decide what kind of voice you want your spouse to hear. You can choose a kind voice that supports and encourages your spouse or another not so positive voice. You can choose a silent voice or a gruff voice that discourages, degrades, and minimizes your spouse on a regular basis. Make the right choice, and shower your spouse with your kindness.

As you choose a love agreement of kindness, it will show up in your spoken words. The words you respond with, the spirit in which they are spoken, and the intentional planting of kindness can become not only a lifestyle but also your heart.

I can tell you that being next to a kind heart is a warm feeling. As your heart becomes kind, your words become kind as well. As your words become kind, your spouse's heart—and yours—will be impacted to become more kind.

A kind touch

Sometimes kindness is spoken more loudly by a touch than by any words you speak. Holding your spouse's hand gently can express volumes of kindness. A gentle caress or light back scratching can be felt as a kind affirmation of your spouse. A foot or back rub in private can really send a message of kindness toward your spouse.

Let me clarify that this is touch for the express purpose of communicating kindness. This is not a touch motivated by or with any hint of sexuality. That kind of touch is called *foreplay*. I think we all know the difference between just stroking your spouse's hair and stroking him or her in an erotic fashion.

When you are expressing kindness with your touch, stay away from his or her sexual areas. Keep your heart pure, and don't be motivated to receive. Don't have the attitude "I'll scratch your back, and you scratch mine." A touch of kindness is motivated purely *to give,* not to receive.

I am not in any way saying that the erotic touch or even a touch motivated for some reciprocation is wrong or sinful. That type of touching is wonderful and very much to be enjoyed. But in this section we are talking about the touch of kindness.

Sowing this type of unselfish, gentle, soft, soothing touch is a great resource for planting kindness into your spouse's heart. Some people might deflect or discount your verbal comments of kindness. Touch is rarely rejected.

Think for a moment about couples you have observed in church. When a husband or wife is touching or scratching the back of his spouse, have you ever seen the spouse jerk away or refuse this touch? Probably not. More often than not, I have seen the spouse move closer into this touch of kindness.

Stop for a moment and think about a kind touch you have received from your spouse. Where were you? How did you feel? You can give that feeling to your spouse at will because you possess the power of kindness. The power of kindness momentarily removes the entire world and its cares from your life, allowing you to drink in pure love from your spouse.

Sowing the kindness of touch is great fun. I encourage you to plant the seed of a kind touch regularly and intentionally upon your spouse. Remember that kindness is a seed that will grow.

The kindness of "teamfulness"

Teamfulness is a word that I have coined to define the way a husband and wife operate in unity with team spirit. Marriage is a team sport. You and your spouse are on the same team. You will have the greatest success if you think and act like a team.

Watching a team championship game in any sport is absolutely amazing. The team members think ahead to anticipate each other's actions. They know the strengths and weakness of each player and capitalize on each member's strengths for the good of the team.

A great team has what I term *teamfulness*. Like the famous three musketeers of old, the team lives "one for all, and all for one." Teamfulness is both an attitude and a behavior.

An attitude of teamfulness is, "We all win together or lose together." In a team in marriage, it is not possible for one team member to win and the other to lose; both people in the team—the whole team—either wins or loses. It's all win or all lose.

Teamfulness as a behavior is a real act of kindness. Here is how teamfulness works in a marriage. When you see the laundry, you do the laundry, because you're part of the team. If you see a situation that must be dealt with regarding one of your children, you handle it without passing it on to your spouse. You know your spouse's schedule, and you cover for him or her without an attitude.

Teamfulness is kindness. It's a way of saying, "I see and anticipate your need, and I'm here for you." Kindness that is expressed through teamfulness is great.

Few things express kindness better than when you realize you forgot the children's gear for their activity, and before you can even contact your spouse for help, your spouse calls to say, "I have the gear, and I'm putting it in your car so you don't have to go all the way home for it . . . love ya." That type of kindness is so timely.

In the same way, your spouse—the other team member—is so in touch with your world that he or she sees the need at times before you do. In this way your spouse throws you the ball, so to speak, and you both score. Then the whole team wins!

Take a moment and see if you can pull up a memory when your spouse expressed kind teamfulness. I imagine you felt *safe,* a part of a team, and successful through the support of the other team member. That's teamfulness, and you can utilize this power of kindness on your spouse.

Intentional kindness

Kindness is something we can do intentionally. Much of what we do in life can be done intentionally. Imagine if your spouse woke up in the morning and prayed, "Lord, help me to be kind to my spouse. Give me eyes to see Your opportunity to plant kindness today. I want my spouse to taste Your fruit of kindness today through me."

Then throughout the day your spouse brings you your favorite beverage, holds your hand, responds to you kindly and, more softly than normal, shows you he or she really cares about what you say and do. He or she offers to take the children to their events and encourages you to just relax. Before he or she leaves with the children, the dishes and kitchen are cleaned so you are not left at home with housework to do. Can you imagine a day like that?

It might feel to you as though you were married to Jesus. What a life! That is the kind of kindness you can intentionally give to your spouse every day. For example, there is one act of intentional kindness that I regularly advise the husbands I counsel to give to their wives. I suggest the same to you. Your wife needs a regular time to relax or play, a time when she does not have to be a mom, a wife, a cook, the clean-up crew, and the leader of bedtime rituals. You can make it possible for her to be away from the home at least one night a week, a time just for her, however she chooses to spend it. This is an intentional act of kindness your wife will greatly appreciate.

If you are a woman, you can plan an intentional act of kindness for your husband, one based on his interests.

Some spouses are extremely gifted in the area of cooking. When they cook, their presentations are exceptional, the fragrances are inviting, the textures and temperatures are varied, and the sauces are exquisite. Maybe this describes you. But in today's busy life-styles, perhaps you don't use that gift very often, settling instead for hurried meals that are easy to prepare. For you, an act of intentional kindness could be scheduling a specific time to prepare a gourmet meal for your family. Maybe you can select one day a week to cook up a storm. You are making a decision to express intentional kindness through your gift of cooking.

I encourage you to plan these intentional acts of kindness. Take a moment and think of at least five ways you can be intentionally kind. You can list them here:

1. _____

2. _____

3. _____

4. _____

5. _____

You see, kindness is in you. Intentional kindness is actively planning to let this kindness out on a regular basis. Being intentional is not only acceptable but also very much appreciated. If I am intentional in my kindness toward Lisa, I am choosing to feed her a meal of kindness. When I plan for her to have a night out, or I do a task for her, I am practicing team behavior toward her.

Spontaneous kindness

We also need to recognize the importance of *spontaneous kindness*. Everyone likes a planned meal, but a surprise one is also appreciated.

Don't become so mechanical in your plans for kindness that you fail to capitalize on those great daily opportunities that come along. If I am watching for opportunities to be kind to Lisa, not a single day will pass without a chance to express spontaneous kindness to her. There is always something. For instance, recently both our children were participating in a huge Easter production at the church called "The Thorn." This production had a five-hundred-member cast. On a particular day at the rehearsal, Hadassah wasn't feeling well. But she still needed to complete a project for school after the rehearsal. So I saw the opportunity to be spontaneously kind. Hadassah and I left the rehearsal and went home where she was able to complete her project. And I got her to bed earlier than if she had stayed at the rehearsal.

Lisa is regularly kind to me. When I come home on a warm day, I first like to spend about fifteen minutes on the hammock in our back yard. It's magical the way both my soul and body get relaxed and refreshed. Lisa usually protects this time so I am not interrupted. This is a spontaneous act of kindness from Lisa's tree of kindness that I get to taste.

My Commitment to Kindness

The first step in making a love agreement of kindness starts like all the other love agreements—by breaking previous agreements. Clear the way for a great foundation for your new agreement by praying this prayer:

> *Jesus, I ask You to forgive me of all acts, attitudes, or beliefs that have been unkind to my spouse. I confess unkindness as a sin against You and my spouse. Please forgive me. I break, in the name of Jesus, any spirit, soul, or body agreements with unkindness. Thank You, Jesus, for hearing my prayer, in Your name.*

Now you are ready to take the next step in your love agreement of kindness by officially declaring your love agreement of kindness.

I WILL BE KIND TO MY SPOUSE,
ELIMINATING ANY TRACE OF MEANNESS
FROM MY BEHAVIOR AND SPEECH.

Pray the following aloud:

In the name of Jesus, I am making a love agreement of kindness toward my spouse. I command all of my mind, will, and emotions to create new beliefs, attitudes, and behaviors to carry out this love agreement. I command that I will see and respond to intentional or spontaneous opportunities for kindness, in the name of Jesus.

GOALS FOR KINDNESS

As in all of the previous love agreements, I want you to be as successful as possible. So set some goals in the area of being kind to your spouse. Underline the goals you are willing to make a commitment to keep, and for each goal you underline, fill in the specific behavior you will use to reach that goal.

SETTING YOUR GOALS

- I will evaluate daily the level of kindness with which I respond to my spouse.

  _____

- I will actually practice two or three kinds of responses.

  _____

- I will daily tell my spouse of one or more acts of kindness that I have noticed my spouse make toward me.

  _____

- I will keep track of the frequency with which I do spontaneous acts of kindness for my spouse.

  _____

- I will plan to touch my spouse in a kind manner on a daily basis.

  _____

- I will measure my kind touches for one month.

  _____

- I will make a list of ways I can express more teamful behavior toward my spouse.

DON'T FORGET TO MEASURE

Now that you have made some goals to be kind, make some form of measurement to keep track of your progress. Your measure can be as simple as sticking up a piece of paper on a mirror with your goals stated. Record your progress regularly so you have an honest account of your efforts. Keep this paper in a handy place so you can review it daily or regularly.

Also, touch bases with your accountability partner regularly. Go over your progress or lack of progress. Pray, laugh, and be encouraged as you direct your life to improve your marriage.

Kindness is a great love agreement to make with yourself. As you wield the power of kindness you will see frowns turn into smiles, snarls turn into *thank yous*, and many other miracles. Remember that change will not happen in a day, but a harvest is assured to those who plant the varied seeds of kindness.

LOVE AGREEMENT #7

I will appreciate my spouse's gifts

and attributes and celebrate

them personally and publicly.

Chapter Nine

Love Agreement #7:
CELEBRATION

Celebration is one of the characteristics of God that I love
the most. Our God is a *celebrator*. He could have made the
world all one color, but, no, He celebrates His creation with endless
amounts of color. All you have to do is drive upstate New York in
the fall to see the splendor of color.

He could have made only humans, but instead He celebrated
life by making all kinds of animals, birds, insects, and our swim-
ming friends. Look at our fabulous foods and all the incredible celebration of bounty that is a part of the very heart of God.

God loves to party. He began His ministry by attending a wedding feast. And remember that all of us who are saved by the blood
of Jesus are invited to a wedding feast. I can't imagine what the God
of all creation does to throw a party, and I can't wait to see!

Celebration is the nature of God. We can understand this better by taking a look at some scenes in the New Testament where we see God the Father and Jesus His Son in the same photograph.

In Matthew 3 we see Jesus getting baptized by his cousin John the Baptist. Besides John and Jesus, there were a number of onlookers at this special event. One very special onlooker at the baptism of Jesus was God the Father. I am sure it was a very exciting moment for the Father as the Son began to step into His destiny in time and space.

God was so excited that He jumped right into time and space with Jesus and all the other onlookers. Look at what God the Father said on that occasion: "This is my Son, whom I love; with him I am well pleased" (Matt. 3:17). In our vernacular, it would have sounded something like, "Look at my Boy; I am so proud of Him."

I find it interesting that God didn't just keep this event a private moment between just John, Jesus, and Himself. No, God celebrated—right there in front of everybody.

Jesus' baptism isn't the only example of God the Father celebrating Jesus. At the moment of Jesus' transfiguration on the mountaintop, God the Father celebrated Jesus in front of some of the disciples. (See Matthew 17:1–13.) Once again, He affirmed Jesus publicly. This time He said the same thing but then added an instruction for the disciples who were observing this celebration: "Listen to him!" (v. 5).

God celebrates! That's just who He is. God has been celebrating you your entire life. He beholds you when you're sleeping; He observes your successes and learning curves with celebration.

If you are a parent, you probably can relate to God's celebratory spirit. Think back to the time when your toddler was learning to draw or paint. No doubt you actually did not have a clue what your child had drawn or painted. Yet, you fawned over your child, exclaiming, "That's great; as a matter of fact I think that's the best painting I have ever seen." You celebrated the drawing proudly by placing it on that family "altar" called the refrigerator.

In just the same way, God responds to your most brilliant and even your less-than-brilliant ideas. He loves you, and He is very committed to celebrating you.

If you grew up without receiving much celebration, the idea that God celebrates you may seem so unfamiliar. It is important for you to know that regardless of who you are or how you grew up, God is a celebrator, and He is celebrating you.

You are not the only one He celebrates. He actually celebrates each of us. This includes the way He celebrates your spouse. Your spouse is the apple of His eye. He listens to his or her breath while asleep and smiles as your spouse goes through the day. He communicates His celebration of your spouse to him or her constantly.

That's why the love agreement of celebration is so important. When you are celebrating your spouse, you are in agreement with God. You are exhibiting your Christlikeness when you are singing the same song of celebration over your spouse that God sings.

WHAT'S TO CELEBRATE?

If you have been married awhile, the song you once sang about your spouse may have grown quiet, distant, and possibly infrequent. Stop for a moment to remember the days when you first met your spouse. Recall those great days of celebration and pleasure.

Back then you didn't need a sermon, self-help book, or a conference to encourage you to celebrate your spouse. You told almost everyone you met the good news about this wonderful new person you had found to celebrate life with. Think about the first time you told your family and friends how smart, attractive, spiritual, or funny this new person was.

That person was the bread of life for you! He or she was the probable solution to your singleness—the one you were waiting for. Take a moment to feel that old feeling. Close your eyes, and remember the song of celebration you once had for your spouse.

Now the years have gone by, and both of you have matured and changed. But it is always a good thing to remember where the song began. I'll never forget the first day I finally met Lisa. We went to the same church and would look at each other, but there never seemed to be an appropriate way to be introduced. She was beautiful, and I definitely wanted to get to know her.

Then the day of destiny happened. I was taking a lunch break from work and walked over to a Christian bookstore to browse around. There she was, standing there. I introduced myself, and I invited her to a pizza place close by—it was there my song began.

She was mature, smart, and had a great spiritual legacy. She was godly and . . . oh, yeah . . . *she was beautiful as well.* She had big green eyes. She was athletic and very responsible. I sang her praises to my roommate, friends, and family.

To this day, Lisa is worthy of celebration. I celebrate her in front of our children, in front of her family, and in front of my family. I celebrate her to our friends and captive audiences at conferences and television. I celebrate her in this book to you.

Not only do I celebrate Lisa, but also, without a doubt, I know that God celebrates my wife. I just want to celebrate with Him who Lisa is. We have stressful days filled with busy schedules and change, but she knows she is celebrated.

Pause for just a moment; does your spouse feel celebrated? Would he or she be able to say, "My spouse celebrates me so much"?

Don't be tempted to slide into a little, "What about me? My spouse doesn't celebrate me." Instead, you lead in the party to celebrate your spouse. Choose to plant celebration in your spouse's life. Everyone loves a party! Once you start the love agreement of celebration, the atmosphere of your relationship has some change—and that's the change in you. You will change and begin to pick up, maintain, or make louder the celebration of your spouse.

It may be that some of those great characteristics in your spouse about which you bragged before marriage may have begun to appear as weaknesses. Before marriage you may have thought your spouse was *thrifty*, but now you call it *cheap*. Once you thought your spouse to be so *smart*, but now it comes off as a *know-it-all*. By now I'm sure the list could go on and on about the weaknesses you see in your spouse.

Think honestly about this: *Has your spouse changed so much, or has the way you think about your spouse changed?* With many couples, it is *how we think about our spouse* that has changed more than the changes in our spouse. We go from a spirit of celebration to a spirit of criticism toward our spouses.

Remember that criticism of another believer in Christ will probably place you on the wrong side of God. He is not a criticizer of your spouse but a celebrator. I like to always be on the same team as God. If I continue to celebrate Lisa, regardless of her disposition or actions, I am in agreement with God.

How Do I Celebrate My Spouse?

Let's consider some ways you can celebrate your spouse.

To the Father

One of the greatest ways to celebrate your spouse is in the presence of his or her Creator. Spend time on a regular basis just praising God for your spouse.

Celebrate the fact that God gave your spouse to you. You can praise Him for how blessed and different you are because your spouse is in your life. Praise God for his or her attractiveness, sexuality, personality, humor, friendship, and any other attributes you want to highlight to the Father.

Remember that God is not only your Father—He is also your Father-in-law. Now I don't know about for you, but if I start bragging about my wife in front of her earthly father, he smiles. One day I was talking to my father-in-law, Harold, about Lisa, and he made a remark that has stuck with me for the nineteen years of our marriage. He smiled at me and said, "I did it all for you." Until I had my own children, I didn't realize the importance of his words. Parents go through years of homework, play, vacations, sickness, school activities, and more to hand over their precious child to another young person whom they barely know.

I know that if a human father-in-law likes to hear good things about their children, so does your heavenly Father-in-law. He loves to hear you praise Him for your spouse. Try it sometime.

In fact, try it right now. Put down this book, and, for the next two or three minutes, get alone and thank God for your spouse. Celebrate your spouse before the living God. See what happens.

If you stopped and praised God, I'll bet you can feel His smile. I always feel His smile when I praise Him for Lisa.

To the enemy

I know I have your attention. What could I possibly mean when I say to celebrate your spouse in front of the enemy? When I say the enemy, I mean the devil and any of his demons that might want to highlight your spouse's weaknesses.

They start by suggesting negative thinking about your spouse. You know the mantra, "Your spouse is selfish, insensitive to your needs, lazy, arrogant, willful, and rebellious." The list never seems to stop. The enemy's objective is to utilize your relationship with your spouse to cause you to hurt, criticize, or emotionally abandon him or her. The enemy knows that your spouse is the closest person to your heart. If he can get you to buy into his lies and criticisms, *whammo,* his work is done; your creativity and resources take over, and you begin to belittle and demean your spouse yourself.

According to the Bible, the devil is the accuser or criticizer of those who are saved (Rev. 12:10–11). Never forget that the enemy hates your godly spouse and the other parent of your children, because together you are raising godly seed for the future battles of the kingdom.

I have learned that the best way to deal with the enemy's lies to me about my spouse is to celebrate her continually. I can recall when I first learned the power of the love agreement of celebration. Aware of the enemy's tactics, I actually made a list of five things that I really loved about Lisa. Each time the enemy started accusing Lisa to me, I would confess these five celebration aspects about Lisa aloud. I continued my vocal celebrations until I was so grateful and more in love with Lisa than before the enemy's attack.

I am sure that during those days I came home particularly glad to see Lisa and she didn't understand why. She was totally unaware of the battle that just occurred. She was also unaware that I won the battle. Because I did achieve the victory, my prize became the fact that I was able to keep a pure, positive, godly perspective about Lisa.

As with all the other love agreements, there is great power in the love agreement to celebrate your spouse. You can utilize this power to fight *for* your spouse instead of *against* him or her, and you will truly be a winner at marriage.

To others

Celebration in the presence of others is powerful. Celebrate your spouse in front of everyone. Your spouse is wonderful; that's why someone as smart as you married him or her. Tell your children privately and publicly in front of your spouse what you like, love, admire, appreciate, and depend upon in your spouse. Let your spouse and your children know that you benefit greatly because your spouse is alive and married to you.

Tell your parents, their parents, your neighbors, and friends about the goodness and value of your spouse. Do this when you are alone with these people. Make others believe that you are blessed because you are married to your spouse.

Dust off that old song you used to sing about your spouse. Sing your spouse's value proudly and loudly. He or she is worth the celebration. You are the president of your spouse's fan club, so let others know about the ongoing celebration of your spouse.

To your spouse

Have you ever heard the story of a parent who told everyone else how wonderful his child was but never told his child? The child never heard the celebration of his father about himself. Sad to say, some of us are good at praising our spouse around others but not as good at celebrating our spouse directly to him or her. Celebrating your spouse directly is a very important aspect of celebration.

There are many different ways to celebrate your spouse. A simple way to begin is to celebrate with gifts. These can be very simple, inexpensive gifts of celebration. You don't always have to spend hundreds or thousands of dollars to celebrate your spouse.

You can celebrate your spouse with consistent, little gifts to demonstrate your love and appreciation. At times a handwritten card is the best way to celebrate your spouse. Surprise him or her with a favorite coffee, tea, juice, or soft drink. Take your spouse to a favorite restaurant for a long lunch.

If your spouse enjoys a massage, buy a gift certificate for one. If sports are a favorite pastime, get some tickets to a sporting event with your spouse's favorite team. These are just a few of the ways you can celebrate your spouse with gifts.

Another way to send a clear message of celebration is with time. Now I don't mean plopping down in front of the TV together or being in the same room together. I mean spending *quality time together* doing something your spouse really likes to do.

Lisa and I have friends, Bill and Patti, who are our children's godparents. Patti really likes teddy bears. She collects them, makes them, and knows the world's best bear makers' names and products. Every year there is a national stuffed bear festival, and one of the ways that Bill celebrates Patti is by going to the festival with her.

Spending time together with your spouse doing the hobbies or activities your spouse enjoys sends a clear message that you really celebrate this aspect about him or her. If your spouse loves to ski, even if you are not a great skier you can go, drink hot chocolate, and listen to the ski stories as a way of celebrating how God made your spouse.

Another very important way to celebrate your spouse is through your spoken words. It would be hard to overestimate the power of your words. To prepare to celebrate your spouse with your words, on the lines below list several things you like about your spouse.

WHAT I LIKE ABOUT MY SPOUSE

1. _____

2. _____

3. _____

4. _____

5. _____

6. _____

7. _____

8. _____

9. _____

10. _____

Many of the things on this list will be things you can use to celebrate your spouse in his or her hearing through your spoken words. Find a way to articulate each thing on the list to your spouse. For example, if you listed that you like your spouse's work ethic, you could say, "You know, I was thinking about you today, and I realized again how industrious you are. You really like to accomplish things, and I really like that about you."

Wouldn't you like to hear your spouse celebrate *you* with those words? Wouldn't that be great? Start the party and celebrate your spouse verbally. For each of the things you listed in the list above, now write a corresponding sentence of celebration that you can express to your spouse.

1. _____

_____

2. _____

_____

3. _____

_____

4. _____

_____

5. _____

_____

6. _____

_____

7. _____

_____

8. _____

_____

9. _____

_____

10. _____

_____

To yourself

That's right; a little bird told me that you talk to yourself. Well, not exactly. But I talk to myself, and most people I know have a little self-dialogue going on also. You know, those little thoughts you have about others but don't speak to them about.

This is where celebration can become really important. This is a really good way to keep your celebration of your spouse going. Stop for a moment and evaluate some ways that God has made your spouse *better* than you. Just as there are some strengths that you have that your spouse does not have, so too he or she will have strengths that you do not have.

For example, Lisa is innately better at instantly discerning the children's medical needs. She is much better at details globally than

I am. Details are very frustrating to me, so I celebrate her strength in this specific area.

Think about some ways in which God made your spouse better than you. List some of these strengths on the lines below.

My Spouse Is Better Than Me

1. _____
2. _____
3. _____
4. _____
5. _____
6. _____
7. _____
8. _____
9. _____
10. _____

If you cannot think of strengths to list, you may need to make celebration of your spouse a priority in your life. When you have a cold, it is hard to taste food or smell the beautiful fragrances in front of you, but that doesn't mean there is something wrong with the food or flowers. So try hard, dig deep, and fill out ten ways that your spouse is better than you.

The fact that your spouse is better than you in specific areas doesn't take away from the wonderful strengths that you possess. It just helps you to focus on your spouse and his or her own wonderful qualities.

I find that keeping this list around until it gets into the heart is helpful. When you can see your spouse's strengths, it is much easier to celebrate your spouse both to yourself, God, others, and the enemy.

Now you are armed with the power of celebration. You can make a love agreement of celebration that can change the atmosphere and the dynamics in your marriage. You are armed with the power of one in celebration, so let's make this agreement official, shall we?

MY COMMITMENT TO CELEBRATION

Remember to begin by breaking any counter agreements. Pray this prayer aloud:

Jesus, I ask for Your forgiveness for any attitudes, beliefs, or behaviors that have been against celebrating my spouse. These attitudes, beliefs, and behaviors are sin, and I repent of these sins. Thank You for Your forgiveness of these sins, in Jesus' name.

You can now proceed to make your love agreement to celebration official.

I WILL APPRECIATE MY SPOUSE'S GIFTS AND
ATTRIBUTES
AND CELEBRATE THEM PERSONALLY AND PUBLICLY.

Go ahead and read the following prayer aloud:

Jesus, I come before You, and I make a love agreement to celebrate my spouse. I agree to celebrate my spouse as You, his or her Creator, celebrate him or her. I command my mind, will, and emotions to create new beliefs, attitudes, and behaviors to cause me to celebrate the great person that my spouse is in Your image. I thank You, Jesus, for giving my spouse to me to celebrate over the course of the rest of my life.

SETTING YOUR GOALS

As in any love agreement, the declaration is only one step in the process. Set your goals for celebrating your spouse. Remember, you get to celebrate him or her for the rest of your life.

Underline the goals you are willing to make a commitment to keep, and for each goal you underline, fill in the specific behavior you will use to reach that goal.

POSSIBLE GOALS

- I will set a time once a week to pray in thanksgiving to God for my spouse.

  _____

- I will intentionally praise my spouse in front of our children.

  _____

- I will intentionally praise my spouse in front of our families.

  _____

- I will intentionally praise my spouse in front of our friends.

  _____

- I will intentionally praise my spouse in front of the enemy.

  _____

- I will memorize the better-than-me list that I prepared earlier in the chapter.

  _____

- I will record how many celebrations I give verbally to my spouse each day.

  _____

- I will also record the number of criticisms I give my spouse daily.

  _____

- I will plan something my spouse would enjoy that celebrates him or her.

  _____

- I will intentionally give gifts to my spouse as an act of celebration.

  _____

DON'T FORGET TO MEASURE YOUR PROGRESS

It's great that you have some goals to enact your love agreement of celebration. These goals can help you move from theory to practice. Remember the only theology you believe is the theology you behave.

So it's time for sticking up notes or paper again. Write your specific behavioral goals to increase celebration in your life toward your spouse. Keep your documentation for your progress available on a regular basis.

Get your accountability partner involved. Go over your results regularly. Yes, this will be work, but there is a harvest for you if you do not give up.

You have the gift and nature of celebration in you already, if you have accepted Jesus Christ as your Savior. The Spirit of God, resident within you, is the spirit of celebration. This spirit loves, gets pleasure from, and looks forward to celebration. Let this great spirit in you hear you cry out in celebration toward your spouse. (If you have not accepted Jesus Christ as your Savior, stop now and ask Him to forgive you for your sins, and to come and live within you so that you can have His spirit of celebration living within. It's the best decision you will ever make.)

Get in on the song of celebration that is already being sung to your spouse. God the Father, the angels, the witnesses in heaven all are celebrating the godly seed your spouse is. Don't let heaven have all the fun—join the celebration! Get ecstatic about your spouse!

Committing to the love agreements of

faithfulness, patience, forgiveness, service,

respect, kindness, and celebration

are your practical strategies for

winning the war of love.

Chapter Ten

THE WAR OF LOVE

Maybe you have been married for some time. You may even say that your marriage experience has been a quiet, peaceful, noneventful, nonconfrontational bed of roses. Well, that's not exactly the case for all of us, and that's the beauty of relationships.

God knew that most of us would experience disturbances, disruptions, or conflict in our relationship with others—and with our spouses. These are the very elements that allow us opportunities for growth. These can be opportunities to evaluate your heart and, hopefully, to mature you further into the image of Christ. Unfortunately, some people do not use these challenging opportunities in life and relationships to mature but instead become harder in their hearts.

Pain comes with life and relationships. Pain is an intended part of the process for us to become Christlike. Many people, including some Christians, have a bizarre notion that life as a Christian was meant to be painless. From my perspective as a counselor, I can tell you that the people I have met who were the most unhealthy emotionally were those trying to avoid pain.

For whatever reason, these unhealthy people are trying to escape the pain of the past, current pain, and pain they fear will come in the future. That's just not reality. Reality is acknowledging the fact that you may have been hurt in the past and will probably have pain of some kind in the present or future.

Healthy people accept pain as a part of life. They know the question is not *if* but *when* pain comes into their lives. Now, I don't suggest you go looking for pain or that you develop a "woe is me" attitude about life. But it would be wise to acknowledge the presence of pain in your life—past, present, and future.

Think for a moment about the various relationships you have been in, including parent/child, husband/wife, teacher/student, peer, family, or romantic relationships. All relationships that are human have pain. What makes all the difference in our lives is whether or not we deal with the pain by choosing to work through it to keep the relationship solvent.

Marriage is a relationship. Most likely your spouse has disappointed you in the past—and will disappoint you in the future. That's life. You have probably caused some disappointment to your spouse also. Once you accept this, you will no longer respond to pain as a personal affront. This inherent conflict in marriage is part of the process I call *the war of love*.

If you are married, you are engaged in this war of love. That doesn't mean that your spouse is the enemy and that you are on the side of justice. No, the war is not about right or wrong—it's about being Christlike and seeking the truth as an opportunity to grow.

The love agreements are part of the war of love. These love agreements are very powerful weapons for you to use to win the war of love. You see, you must understand this powerful biblical principle: *If you love, love never fails.* (See 1 Corinthians 13:8.) I like the fact that love never fails, even though I know that I can fail. This knowledge assures me that if I can love, I will learn to fail less and less and will someday win the war of love.

Love is the cornerstone of marriage. The one who loves, wins the war. Committing to the love agreements of faithfulness, patience, forgiveness, service, respect, kindness, and celebration are your practical strategies for winning the war of love.

There is no doubt that some days you will find yourself in a battle to love when you feel hurt, misunderstood, tired, or just want to lash out at your spouse. But because of Christ and your love for Him and the love you have for your spouse, making your love agreements practical, measurable, and accountable will give you a much better likelihood of winning than if you ignore the problematic issues in your marriage and attempt to keep love ethereal and intangible. The love agreements give you tools for wrapping your hands around your marriage and moving it out of the war of love.

PREPARE YOUR BATTLE STRATEGIES

There are some battle strategies that you can use to be successful in your journey through the love agreements.

For a moment, let's go back in history to a dreadful but brilliant military tactician. Adolph Hitler was definitely an evil person driven by some very bizarre and ungodly motives. He, however, introduced a brilliant military strategy that almost allowed him to conquer an unlimited number of nations.

Stay with me here, as I am talking about strategy. He introduced the war technique of the *blitzkrieg*. A blitzkrieg was a simple, powerful, and very effective technique of war. The blitzkrieg technique enabled Hitler's armies to blow through Europe conquering the enemy wherever the troops set foot. In essence, the blitzkrieg tactic used by Hitler was a style of warfare completely opposite to the tactic of positioning troops in trenches to maintain the lines of battle. That style of warfare condemned armies to practical uselessness.[1] Instead, Hitler put all his armed forces, planes, tanks, and soldiers concentrated like a laser in one direction with one front at a time, moving through the land like an arm sweeping across a table.

So why didn't Hitler win the war in the end? Simple—he changed strategies. In the end, he split his forces to fight the United States and England on one side and Russia on the other. He divided his resources and was defeated.

What does all this war stuff have to do with the love agreements we have described in this book? *Everything.*

You see, if you generally try to be more kind or to serve your spouse more your way, you may not get long-term results. You will be like the soldiers stuck in trenches far from where the battle is taking place. Your ways may be useless for accomplishing the goals you have set for each of your love agreements. A much better plan is to work at your love agreements in the blitzkrieg method.

Take all your effort and focus it on one love agreement. Suppose you are working on the love agreement of kindness. Choose one of your goals in the kindness love agreement and stay focused, measuring your progress. Stay consistent in your goal of kindness until you think you have achieved your goal. Then take on another goal of kindness. Measure that goal, and stay in blitzkrieg mode until you have achieved each goal you set for yourself.

Now you are going to see some real results in your war of love. You will be able to see the measurements you logged showing proof that you are actually much kinder today than you were weeks or months ago. Your written notes demonstrate your strategies and the victories you have won.

The love agreements are blitzkrieg tactics assuring your success. You are not attacking all fronts at all times but have isolated your efforts to one front at a time. As you secure an area like kindness and hold that ground successfully for a time, then you can move on to the next love agreement or goal.

In this way you have the practice, discipline, focus, and determination you need to take another part of your territory in the war of love.

Due to changing your behavior from your old *trench tactics*, your spouse is forced to face a growth opportunity. There may be times when he or she faces this new opportunity graciously. But at other times your change may create real conflict.

For example, suppose in your marriage you previously didn't serve your spouse well by doing things around the house. Your lack of service in this area has created a "trench tactic" system, causing your spouse to harbor resentment. You also created an anger-producing situation for your spouse each time the subject of your lack of helpfulness came up. The shame that would produce in you would distract you from whatever issue you were trying to discuss.

However, with your blitzkrieg maneuver, you have been serving your spouse consistently for several months. Now you are winning the war of love. Your spouse's counterattack of trying to shame and distract you is no longer effective. Obviously it is no longer true that you are not helpful. As a result, your spouse now has an opportunity to grow out of the resentment and anger you formerly caused.

I remember a blitzkrieg Lisa did on me, and it totally shut me up ever since. Remember, my wife is almost perfect with very few flaws at all. Early in our marriage, Lisa had a habit of misplacing her keys. We would both spend time repeatedly looking for those keys. Periodically I would bring this up (see I'm not perfect). So one time I brought this up kiddingly, and Lisa challenged me to remember the last time she had lost her keys. I really couldn't remember; it must have been several years, possibly more than five years since I remembered a time when she lost her keys.

She had *blitzkrieged* me. Years earlier she had fixed this issue. She stayed consistent, and in one blow she was able to win a war of love. I had nothing to say about her losing her keys anymore, and I haven't brought it up since. My wife's change of behavior faced me with an opportunity for growth.

The changes that you make probably will cause some conflict—battle skirmishes. Conflict is inevitable and guaranteed in a marriage relationship if you are actively and intentionally changing from your former "trench tactics" to the more effective "blitzkrieg tactics." When conflict comes, patiently stay consistent. Your consistency is crucial for you to ultimately win the war of love.

Your consistency will bring results. In Galatians 6:9 we read: "Let us not become weary in *doing good*, for at the proper time we will reap a harvest if we do not give up" (emphasis added).

Your love agreements will reap a harvest if you don't give up. I can't think of anything better than trying to love your spouse more than before. Like a harvest, there is a season of planting and then a season of harvest. As Americans we tend to want an "instant harvest." You know, the kind of harvest where you plant the seed today and eat the fruit tomorrow. Unfortunately God has not created such a process. A harvest takes time and nurturing.

It will take time for your spouse to trust any new behavior. As time and consistency occur, he or she will begin to trust this new behavior. For some behaviors it may take quite a while for your spouse to trust that you have actually and sincerely changed. It's at the point of trusting your new behavior that they will decide to change or not. So be patient as you go through the war of love.

Keep It Real

The love agreements are pathways for new growth. You will not be perfect on this road of growth. *Stay real, and avoid the "always" and "never" traps.* Neither you nor I are capable of always being loving or perfect and never being imperfect. This is a growth process.

There will be ups and downs in your growth process. Why do I say this? Because you will need to be patient with yourself as you grow. Some days you will be very successful, and you will feel great. Other days in the war of love you might feel like a failure. You may have tried to be patient and kind or to serve, and you just failed. That's life, and it will probably happen again. Don't worry about losing some of the *battles* in the war of love—your goal is to *win the war!* It's important that you maintain your resolve to continue. You'll have the temptation to give up, just as Jesus did.

I'm sure that somewhere along the path of false accusations, beatings, and crucifixion, Jesus might have been tempted to say, "That's enough!" Yet He never lost sight of His long-term goal: "the joy set before him," which was for our salvation. He continued in the battle until He won the war. I want to encourage you to stay in the war of love because it is worth winning.

One area of concern that could cause you to become weary and discouraged is when you start to get frustrated because your spouse is not appreciating "all the changes" you are implementing. After all, you are really working hard, and you start to feel that even if your spouse is not going to change, he or she should at least notice that you are making such a big effort.

This is a tricky trap. As soon as your motivation moves from pleasing Jesus and trying to be more like Him to needing appreciation from your spouse, you can, and probably will, get disappointed, hurt, and discouraged.

If I want Lisa to praise me for my obvious efforts, I place in her hands the power to decide how I feel about what I am doing.

There have been many times when I would really serve her by putting my agendas to the side and simply serving her needs. At these times, when I expected praise or appreciation, and I received nothing or, even worse, received criticism, I would become frustrated. You see, at that point I had moved from a motivation to please Jesus to playing a game to receive praise from Lisa.

I had to learn to make my actions something between Jesus and me alone instead of something between Lisa and me. Once I did that, it was Jesus' approval that I sought. When I went to the basement and complained to Jesus by saying, "I served all day. I need Your smile," not only would He smile at me, but He would also tell me that He was proud of me. When I made my actions a matter between Jesus and me alone, then He alone was the one to decide if I was appreciated or not.

God is faithful. He loves when I serve Lisa with patience, kindness, and faithfulness—in other words, when I keep my love agreements.

When you fall into self-pity or frustration, it is usually a sign you want appreciation. Don't look to your spouse to fill your cup; look to Jesus. Hear His voice. He knows how to pour praise into an honest heart that is trying to love His child, your spouse.

GO FORWARD

You are about to take a fantastic journey of change. You are on a journey to be more Christlike than ever before. This journey will require radical shifts in your thinking and behavior.

You are now more informed than many on how to honestly change the dynamics in your marriage. You are the power of one who decides if change should occur. In the love agreements you were asked to accept any flaws your spouse might have. You learned to concentrate your attention on yourself in order to become a great influencer in your marriage.

You have been taught the important principle of the power of the seed. You know that the Spirit of God in you is already faithful, patient, forgiving, serving, respectful, kind, and celebrating. This seed is in you.

You just have to let this seed out of you and grow all the fruit that you want your spouse to taste. As he or she tastes over and over the godly fruit hanging on your tree, your spouse will begin to trust that a continual harvest of fruit will be available to him or her.

The love agreements will teach you this critical principle: believe your behavior. As you look at your behavior, you are much more likely to be intentional and successful.

You also learned the importance of having specific goals that you measure consistently. This is a powerful principle in your growth process. As you learn to add accountability to each love agreement, you are almost assured of victory.

Ecclesiastes 4:9–10 reveals the principle that "two are better than one, because they have a good return for their work: If one falls down, his friend can help him up. But pity the man who falls and has no one to help him up!"

As you go into battle, you are not going alone. No army sends a soldier out to battle alone. One of the first things that happen to a recruit in boot camp is for him to be assigned a buddy. His buddy is there to pick him up if he gets wounded, and he is there for his buddy as well.

Be encouraged that this is a great journey. It is a journey you don't have to wait for your spouse to take with you. You take the journey, and maybe your spouse will come along later.

Don't be discouraged; your spouse may not change immediately. If your spouse is not intentionally trying to become more Christlike, it may be a while. He or she may see no need to change and may be content at the level of Christlikeness he or she has reached with little effort. Leave that to Jesus. You just push forward practically and intentionally.

Like a mother eagle, I am at the point of pushing you out of the nest to fly. As you jump and go, you will experience your spiritual wings in a grand new way.

You will soar in Christ like no other time in your life. I live in Colorado, and we go to a place in the mountains where bald eagles live. To watch a bald eagle fly is absolutely amazing. You literally stop what you're doing to watch. You pull your car over and just watch in amazement at the flight of the eagle.

That is what you want your spouse to see in you—the flight of an eagle. Give him or her a chance to see faithfulness, patience, forgiveness, service, respect, kindness, and celebration soaring every day in his or her life.

Your spouse needs to have the time to stop and drink in these experiences of your love agreements. Soar, and let him or her watch. If your spouse chooses to join you in flight, that's great. If not, you are the power of one enticing others to the great flight of becoming more like Jesus.

May God bless your flight.

—DOUGLAS WEISS, PHD

NOTES

CHAPTER 1 • THE LOVE AGREEMENTS

1. Douglas Weiss, *Intimacy: A 100-Day Guide to Better Relationships* (Lake Mary, FL: Siloam, 2001).

CHAPTER 2 • LET'S PRETEND

1. Weiss, *Intimacy*, 231–236.

CHAPTER 3 • LOVE AGREEMENT #1: FAITHFULNESS

1. Weiss, *Intimacy*, 158–168.

CHAPTER 5 • LOVE AGREEMENT #3: FORGIVENESS

1. Weiss, *Intimacy*, 58–62.

2. Ibid.

3. The four exercises regarding self-forgiveness, God's forgiveness, and forgiveness of your spouse are adapted from Doug Weiss, *Intimacy: A 100-Day Guide to Lasting Relationships,* 62–66.

4. Ibid.

5. Ibid.

6. Ibid.

CHAPTER 10 • THE WAR OF LOVE

1. For more information about the blitzkrieg tactics used by Hitler in World War II, see http://www.spartacus.schoolnet.co.uk /2WWblitzkreig.htm.

FOR FURTHER INFORMATION ON THE MINISTRY
OF DR. WEISS:

Visit his Web site at www.drdougweiss.com
E-mail: info@drdougweiss.com
Or call: 719-278-3708
Or write: Heart to Heart Counseling Center
5080 Mark Dabling Blvd.
Colorado Springs, CO 80918

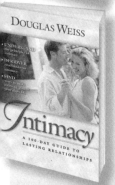

Strang Communications, the publisher of both Charisma House and *Charisma* magazine, wants to give you 3 FREE ISSUES of our award-winning magazine.

Since its inception in 1975, *Charisma* magazine has helped thousands of Christians stay connected with what God is doing worldwide.

Within its pages you will discover in-depth reports and the latest news from a Christian perspective, biblical health tips, global events in the body of Christ, personality profiles, and so much more. Join the family of *Charisma* readers who enjoy feeding their spirit each month with miracle-filled testimonies and inspiring articles that bring clarity, provoke prayer, and demand answers.

To claim your **3 free issues** of *Charisma,* send your name and address to: Charisma 3 Free Issue Offer, 600 Rinehart Road, Lake Mary, FL 32746. Or you may call 1-800-829-3346 and ask for Offer # 93FREE. This offer is only valid in the USA.

---

www.charismamag.com